Yale!

May the thoughts in this book help you win the IRS Coaching Information Game!

Tim Timineri

WINNING THE INFORMATION GAME

SEVEN STEPS TO MARKET DOMINATION

Frederick W. "Tim" Timmerman, Jr.

Executive Excellence Publishing

© 2000 Frederick W. Timmerman, Jr.

All rights reserved. No portion of this book may be reproduced or transmitted in any form or by any means, electronic or mechanical, including photocopying, recording, or by any information storage and retrieval system, without written permission from the publisher, except in the case of brief quotations embodied in critical reviews and certain other noncommercial uses permitted by copyright law.

For permissions requests, contact the publisher at:
Executive Excellence Publishing
1344 East 1120 South
Provo, UT 84606
phone: 1-801-375-4060
toll free: 1-800-304-9782
fax: 1-801-377-5960
www.eep.com

For Executive Excellence books, magazines and other products, contact Executive Excellence directly. Call 1-800-304-9782, fax 1-801-377-5960, or visit our Web site at www.eep.com.

Printed in the United States

10 9 8 7 6 5 4 3 2 1

ISBN 1-890009-76-8

Libary of Congress Catalog Card Number: 99-75748

Cover design by Joe McGovern and Jim Easley

Printed by Publishers Press

*"The timid man yearns for full value
and asks a tenth;
the bold man strikes for double value
and compromises at par."*
—*Mark Twain*

ACKNOWLEDGMENTS

There are many people and organizations I could thank when I look back on the development of this book. Many probably don't have any sense of what they contributed, and that's just the point. The most interesting thing about the evolution of knowledge is that ideas, thoughts and insights are always freely given by those who care. It must be this way if our world is to continue to grow and prosper. Therefore, to those who have shared and to those who have inspired me in so many ways over the years, I acknowledge their help with grateful thanks. In whatever small way, it is my hope that my words recorded here will add a bit more to the body of business knowledge and practice.

To start, a very special thanks to my closest friend and confidant, Lou Csoka. I was and am blessed to have him as a college classmate, lifelong friend, and foil for my many ideas. Moreover, this country is blessed that as a young man he found his way to our shores after fleeing the Russians during the Hungarian uprising in the 50's. We have walked on many beaches together and will walk on many more. I only wish that I had gotten him to co-author this book with me. As an inside practitioner and thinker they don't come any better.

Having a vision is one thing. Turning that vision into reality is quite another. In that regard, writers, friends, and thinkers like Bob Sorley and Wes Roberts stand out. In daring to put their own thoughts down and being willing to take the heat, they give me comfort and courage to write myself. To those who have a sense of history and its implications for the future, especially Paul Ringenbach, author of the magnificent history of USAA, and Don Holder, warrior, patriot, writer, historian, and futurist—my thanks for your enduring support and counsel. To business giants Robert McDermott, Chairman Emeritus, USAA, and his successor at USAA, Bob Herres, my thanks also. They have put a mark on the wall that is sought by many in business but equaled by few.

To the many "tigers" that fortunately still inhabit the business world and who have shared their thoughts with me, my sincere appreciation for the help you have given me. I assure you I will always seek to feed the tigers, ride the horses, and shoot the dogs. I include here business pioneers and partners Bill Hutton, Jim Siegle, Mike Bottema, Steve Kempf, Ron Dill, Paul Root, George Tye, Peter Garcia, and Perry Stevens.

Mentors and leaders give one courage to have heroes, to believe, and to write. I have been fortunate to have had many over the years. Foremost among them are General Colin Powell, General George Blanchard, Joe House, Rick Fowler, and Lou Hightower. They have reminded me that the "harder right" instead of the "easier wrong" is always the way to go and that the pretenders will always be found out.

The friends who have shared, read, and critiqued what I have written are many. Especially noteworthy have been the insights of John O'Neill, Ben Jurewicz, Donna Kirby, John Douglas, Gloria Craven, Jerry Gass, Ed Schrenk, Doris Dent, Bob Logan, Steve Fingland, and Jim Roberts. Other friends who have helped include Jim Ferguson, Stan Polk and Art Pratt. I would also be remiss if I didn't thank the thousands of anonymous people who pass jokes around on the Internet, providing much of the humor and reflection in the pages that follow.

To my current partners at DIRECT1 who share the vision and have the fire to make things happen, especially Gary Rhoads, Scott Smith, Michael Swenson, and David Whitlark—a special thanks for reading, critiquing and making my book better. I have never been privileged to associate with a more forward thinking, innovative group of business professionals. They truly understand the scope of the opportunity presented through companies like DIRECT1 for businesses to take charge of their destinies in the information age.

Organizations rarely get mentioned, but I want to recognize several. First, the United States Military Academy, West Point prepared me for service in a constantly changing world. Second, the US Army allowed me to grow and learn. Then, solid business organizations such as USAA and the Marketing Science Institute gave me the chance to try out new ideas that provide a backdrop of practice to many of the assertions in this book.

Another group that rarely gets recognized are the ones who put a book like this together. To Ken Shelton and his wonderful staff at Executive Excellence Publishing, especially my editor, Ryan Jensen—thanks for believing in the manuscript and helping craft it into a working, readable book.

Finally, on a personal note, thanks to my wife Susan and my wonderful children, Eric, Erin, Tracey, and our special angel "Cindy" for their love and caring. They know there is only one time to leave Dad alone, and that's when he is writing. Their support has been and will continue to be a special source of strength. I end with an expression of gratitude to my mom and dad. The values and the ethics-based sense of perspective we carry forward is a priceless treasure passed on from generation to generation. Such baselines are even more important in the information age, when speed demands an unwavering values base and unshakable ethics.

TABLE OF CONTENTS

Preface 13

Chapter I: Let the Game Begin 17

Chapter II: Win the Battle Within 29

Chapter III: Share the Business Vision...........................41

Chapter IV: Solve the Riddle of the Three I's 53

Chapter V: Understand Information Clearing Houses 69

Chapter VI: Deploy and Use Clearing Houses 87

Chapter VII: Know the Information Principles 111

Chapter VIII: Possess the Needed Skills 125

Chapter IX: Avoid Information Highway Potholes 141

Appendix A (Proactive Vs. Reactive Thinking) 154

Appendix B (Business Characteristics)..........................155

References and Selected Readings 157

Index 163

PREFACE

Although I didn't realize it at the time, my interest in the power of electronic tools and their importance to the process of producing good, timely information actually began in 1964. I was in my junior year as a cadet at West Point and had been selected to learn about a new computing capability embedded in a machine. As we have learned since, it was a technological capability that would come to drive what we now know as the "Information Age."

When I was ushered for the first time into a white, almost completely sterile room in the basement of Thayer Hall, the main academic building at West Point, what I came face to face with was an early version of the machine we now know as a computer. It was a huge baby! The blinking lights and sense of order were overpowering. The impact was unearthly.

The feeling hit me that I was seeing a new being that was going to change the way we collect, integrate, disseminate, and use information. This thought was frightening and uplifting at the same time. It became even more pronounced as we worked with the machine during the following academic semester.

Subsequently, I had occasion to observe the Military's efforts to harness electronic technology as a cavalry officer in Germany. My experiences included work with more advanced versions of the machine I had worked with at West Point. What was exciting was

Winning the Information Game

that we labored to use it to better equip and supply the units facing our enemies of that day across the Iron Curtain.

My experience with these new information tools caused me to have mixed emotions about what I was seeing. I thought I had a vision of the potential they represented. However, those around me went about trying to figure out how to make the technology support the status quo rather than using it as a springboard to innovation and real operational advantage. But junior people do not speak out just because they have mixed emotions. Maybe I was missing something, so I kept quiet.

In 1970, fresh from line combat duty in Vietnam, I returned to Duke University for advanced study on my way to join the West Point faculty. After searing, sometimes heartwrenching experiences driven by our lack of coherent, timely information I was ready to apply myself completely to the task of finding better ways at Duke to acquire, process, and win with information. I had stood many nights in a dark tank turret looking out over the jungle landscape called "Nam" wishing I had the tools to know what my enemy was doing. The newspapers and press said we had the technology to know those things. If so, why didn't I know, and why were my soldiers suffering? I was determined to find out.

At Duke I learned a great deal about theories of human and organizational behavior. I had mixed emotions about some of these theories. What I did learn is that technology will always get you lots of data. The problem is making sense of all that data and making better use of it than your competitor so you win, whether you are on the battlefield or in the business world. That is, taking the feedback and making it work for you.

One of my current business partners recently told me a story that illustrates this point. A company he was advising had just installed Lotus Notes to speed things up and enhance communications. Each employee was supposed to input when and where meetings were to be held, thus reducing the flow of paper. Well, everyone did this, but no one could keep up with what was being posted. The result was something just slightly short of chaos and a lot of missed meetings. Even if people had kept up with what was being posted, the lack of coordination and shear volume of inputs guaranteed business priority gridlock.

After a marvelous experience at West Point teaching, I went back to the active military. I was surprised to find that although the technology had continued to evolve, the people in charge seemed to have stayed the same, remaining frozen in time. Again, I had mixed emotions; however, this time I started writing and speaking up.

Because of an article entitled "Yes, Sir! General Machine, Sir!" a young Lieutenant Colonel received far more attention than he could have ever envisioned. The article was a critique of how the military was applying computer technology. In it, I made the following observation: "The paradox we face today with our current approaches to the employment of computers, statistics, and training simulation technology is that we may well have lost rather than gained in the capability to command and control our forces."

In the intervening years that thought has remained with me. I wrote this book to offer another view and encourage new thinking and new ideas about winning with information. On many days, as we approach a new century, I feel I could substitute the words *businesses* and *companies* in the quote from my 1980s article. It would now read: "The paradox we face today with our current approaches to the employment of computers, statistics, and training simulation technology is that we may well have lost rather than gained in the capability to command and control our businesses and companies."

Businesses are facing nothing less than a revolution, in which many of the players don't have a clue about what's going on. And to make matters worse, staying the same is not an option. I decided to use the idea of winning the information game as a way to lay down some key steps we need to follow in order to cope with the massive changes we are experiencing in the business world. There are lots of "how to" books when it comes to the mechanics and engineering of the process. In contrast, very little has been written about what we business types need to do personally and professionally. This is the gap this book fills.

Winning the Information Game

What we face in business today is a situation that is far different from anything we have ever experienced. The technological revolution really is all about us personally and professionally—how we use information to think, process, and interact with our world. The time has come to stop letting all that data push us around.
FWT, Jr.

CHAPTER I

LET THE GAME BEGIN

*"Learning is not compulsory;
neither is survival."*
—W. Edwards Deming

Stop! Are you tired of being pushed around by ever-increasing volumes of data pulling you and your business in every direction? Do you want to dominate and win the information game in the information-age business world, but things just don't seem to be working out the way you thought? Take heart, you're not alone! Here is some feedback from managers about what is giving them fits and keeping them up at night:

• All those fancy computers, phone systems, and complicated business programs with all their bells and whistles just aren't giving us the return we wanted.

• Our customers are screaming about having to talk to machines rather than people.

• Our employees are turning over faster than a top spinning on a glass coffee table.

• We see the same problems over and over again.

• Nothing seems to get fixed.

• The politics and in-fighting around the company are out of control.

• When are we going to get some real work done around here?

- Who's in charge?—the machines or us?
- Doesn't skill matter any more?

It's really bleak, you think! No one seems to be talking to anyone else. If you hear the word *change* one more time you believe you may choke the sender of the message. You are beginning to hate every consultant that comes through the door with a new idea. You are finding yourself almost liking lawyers. Well, welcome to the Information Age in many companies today!

It's so bad that it was reported on the Internet that when a consultant died recently in a car accident on his 40th birthday he found himself greeted at the pearly gates by a brass band. Saint Peter ran over and shook his hand. "Congratulations!" shouted Saint Peter.

"Congratulations for what?" asked the consultant.

Saint Peter replied, "We're celebrating the fact that you lived to be 160 years old!"

"But, that's not true," replied the consultant. "I only lived to be forty!"

"That's impossible," replied Saint Peter, "We added up all the time sheets you submitted to the businesses you billed."

It's not change, it's a revolution! Our companies and businesses are struggling to harness the potential of an increasingly complex digital word that includes the Internet, computers, databases, fiber optics, and satellites. The problem is that we are using old thinking and old behaviors to do it, and the joke's on us. For example, senators are not allowed to operate portable laptop computers on the Senate floor when it is in session. Why? Because as one venerable senator allegedly remarked, sometimes tradition is more important than progress. This sort of mentality may be appropriate "sometimes," but one of those times is not when it comes to running our businesses.

Today's revolution is not about things and new gadgets. If it were, we would have figured out how to dominate, and we would have been in the business winner's circle long ago. Contrary to our thinking, the revolution is about us and how we think about, act, and use information. The game's up! We need to learn some new behaviors and start doing things differently, if we are to succeed.

That's what this book is all about—developing new ways of thinking so we can get out of our self-created boxes, win the information game, and drive information again. Just how do we use feedback to drive information rather than letting it drive us? Once we figure that out, we can begin to achieve the business results we so ardently desire. Then we will be able to truly dominate our markets with information that supports and promotes results. No longer will we be slaves to the information we receive.

How we think and how we interact in both personal and professional settings depends on feedback—data and signals. What if we weren't ready to deal with its "volume" and "speed" because of the way we think? We might feel stressed and overwhelmed and blame things on change. But what if change isn't the real problem? What if the problem really involved the need for us to broaden ourselves and fundamentally change the ways we acquire, process, and act on the feedback we receive from our environment—in short, to adapt personally, professionally, and organizationally?

When companies call about helping them with information overload, generally we find the problem is not with the systems but with the people using the systems. Too often, we are so fixed on our own small worlds that we can't see the big picture. The problem reminds me of another story going around about three engineers who were driving to an important company meeting when their car suddenly died on the side of the road. There stood an electrical engineer, a chemical engineer and a Microsoft engineer wondering how to deal with the situation.

The electrical engineer suggested that the problem might be in the wiring or the black boxes and recommended stripping down the electronics to find out what was wrong. "No, No, that's not the problem," said the chemical engineer. "It has to be the fuel system. Let's drain it and then replace the gas."

"Both of you don't know what you're talking about," observed the calm, cool Microsoft engineer. "The problem is really very simple.

All we have to do is close all the windows, get out, get back in, open the windows again and we'll all be OK!"

Other revolutions have been about creating new things. If we were to use that yardstick, and step back, we might find that the current age is not all that unique because it was others a while back who developed such things as facsimile machines, television, telephones, automobiles, and airplanes. It may seem simplistic, but all we've really seen since the 1960s has been the evolution of the computer and the growth in our ability to acquire and process information digitally.

If this is anywhere close to being true, then the conclusion must be that this revolution is about us and our ability to develop new ways of taking charge and handling feedback. Put another way, we are up to our collective necks, almost paralyzed, with too much data and not enough useful information! We cry out, and rightly so, for some order and routine. We need some steps, a structure to get out of the information swamp and drive things again using tools that make information work for us.

THE STRUCTURE

The following pages detail seven direct steps that we must take to close the gap between the opportunities afforded us by technology and our own ability to collect, integrate, share, and use information. The goal is market domination through feedback-driven insights about what we can do to win the information game and generate the solutions that foster business success. Here are the seven steps:

Step One: Win the battle within. In chapter two we confront the barriers within ourselves—our assumptions, biases, insecurities—that promote our unwarranted comfort with the status quo.

Step Two: See, understand, and promote a shared business vision. In chapter three the focus turns to understanding that a clear, shared business focus is the key enabler to sustaining the ability to use feedback to do the things we want it to. Without an enduring shared focus, we won't have the will to stay the course and change our behaviors and attitudes. More important, we won't be able to communicate to our businesses what must be done to win and dominate our markets.

Step three: Solve the feedback riddle of acquiring, processing, and using information. Chapter four addresses the importance of three critical external factors that determine our success—Information, Integration, and Interactivity. When I refer to the riddle of the three I's, I'm referring to how we learn to 1) know what information is needed; 2) organize to ensure its systematic collection, processing, and dissemination; 3) orient so as to leverage the power of connecting with our customers.

Step four: Understand, deploy, and use information clearing houses. Information clearing houses are the feedback integration engines needed to drive information and dominate our business worlds. Chapters four and five are devoted to this step. In chapter four, I lay down the model of a clearing house. Chapter five provides practical examples of information clearing houses in action.

Step five: Know and act on critical information principles. Chapter seven contains a detailed discussion of nine principles that we need to know in order to adapt and become accomplished information drivers. Knowing and applying these principles can keep us on track and out of side issues that inhibit and confuse our ability to apply scarce company resources correctly.

Step six: Possess the needed information skills. The technology we use to run our businesses has changed dramatically in recent years; what hasn't kept pace are the skills required of us to effectively manage and lead. Chapter eight addresses the skills each individual needs to master in order to excel.

Step seven: Avoid dangerous potholes along the information highway. In chapter nine, I outline ten potentially fatal mistakes for our businesses. In our quest for a definitive path to market domination we must avoid falling into the potholes that dot the information highway and thereby avoid the fate of many businesses that are no longer a part of the game—becoming roadkill.

SURVIVAL

As my wife and I walked, with our friends of long standing, along the sugar-white sandy beach that harmoniously merged with a placid Gulf of Mexico at the Alabama shore a couple of years back, a thought struck me: "Why can't our companies and businesses act like the school of small fish that were swimming near the shore?" In a seemingly effortless fashion, the school avoided obstacles in its path, flowing around and over impediments, changed direction with precision when danger threatened, and moved to avoid a rock suddenly thrown in its direction almost before it hit the water. Truly the school of fish acted as if it were one rather than a collection of thousands. Moreover, it seemed marvelously anticipatory and orderly in its use of feedback—how powerful, how responsive, and how adaptive!

It was apparent to me then, and still is today, that many late 20th century companies seem frozen in time and are unwilling or unable to change, although disaster is moving closer and closer to their doorsteps. Well-meaning professionals rush from one type of management model to another—today empowerment, tomorrow participative leadership, next week who knows what.

That moment on the beach became the catalyst for me to set down the thoughts of many years that follow in this book. The aim is to create useful stepping stones for all travelers on the business highway of today and tomorrow so that we all can adapt, use feedback to dominate, and become competent information drivers. After all, no one wants to be like Ken Olson, president/chairman and co-founder of Digital Equipment Corporation, who said in 1977, "There is no reason anyone would want a computer in their home."

I hope that you come to this book with the thought that it offers you the step-by-step opportunity to come to grips with your business frustrations. As a reader looking to recharge and reflect, realize that your dissatisfaction should not be with your individual conditions, but rather with your own views of those conditions. We need to realize that the time has come to stop putting up with the seeming inability of everyone to be adaptive and self-correcting in

Let the Game Begin

a world that has never been richer with the opportunity to do so. Our task is to take charge and figure out how to drive information.

THE OPPORTUNITY

One would be a fool to try to predict with absolute certainty what the future holds. But the opportunity that waits is very clear. All rhetoric aside, companies and business professionals have the opportunity to reinvent themselves structurally, organizationally, and humanistically. The feedback tools exist to create the capability to adaptively acquire, process and drive INFORMATION against well-defined and rigorously disciplined organizational visions. Certainly the schools of fish I observed on the Alabama gulf coast functioned in this fashion, even though much of their capability was instinctively embedded—or was it?

This is not so much a "how to" book as it is a "what to do" book. General George Patton once said in the heat of battle, "Tell people what to do, not how to do it, and they will surprise you with their ingenuity." Business battlefields today are no less intense. And even though the competition is economic, the same principle applies. If we can understand what must be done, then it is a matter of each of us mustering the will to step forward and address "how to do it."

CRITICAL CONCEPTS

A number of concepts and terms will be used repeatedly in the following pages. So that you know what I mean when I use them, I want to define three critical concepts at the outset of our discussion.

1. Feedback System. A feedback system is a customized grouping of hardware, supporting software, and people. The goal of the system is focused collection and integration of data and then its dissemination as information to the right user at the right time. It is a total process in which utility and value are established through continuous outputs that promote solutions and results. Collection methods can be both passive and active. In the case of passive collection, it is generally unstructured and anecdotal. Structure is added during the integration phase. An example of passive feedback collection might be an Internet email option where customers are invited to provide any feedback they feel like giving to a business. Active collection, in contrast, is structured from the outset, and integration involves the packaging of the structured input. Surveys where a customer or an employee is asked to fill out a structured form or questionnaire are examples of active feedback collection.

2. Information Clearing House. An information clearing house is a place where people manage the transformation of collected feedback into information that is disseminated to the right user at the right time. It is the feedback to information transformation that is at the heart of the operation, ensuring that everything gets and stays linked together as user needs evolve over time. The primary functions performed in the clearing house are information packaging, analysis if required, timely information dissemination, follow-up, and the sharing of the actions taken in response to the information provided. Because the clearing house depends on a blend of hardware, software, and people for its effectiveness, clearing house managers must understand the hardware and software, manage their own teams, and serve as information facilitators for the user. One clearing house can act as the core for a number of feedback systems as long as each feedback system remains distinct and separate.

3. Data Warehouse. A data warehouse is where the feedback used by the clearing house is stored for immediate or subsequent use. Normally a number of relational databases in the data warehouse support the feedback systems that may be serviced by the information clearing house. Depending on the type of output display system used or the source of the data, it may or may not be certified. The power of the data warehouse resides in its potential to store data over time, providing the basis for effective trending, forecasting, and business learning. In this way, the stage is set for us to drive information.

THE PAYOFF

If we win the information game, what is the payoff? What will we and our information powered companies look like? First, we will succeed by organizing ourselves based on application of a superb blend of business vision, supporting information processing tools, and human craft to achieve proper business success. Then working from the vision, our companies will ensure that their actions are clear and internalized, and everyone will have a picture of what needs to be done to succeed. In support, company leadership will act to ensure that the vision is shared at all levels. Senior management will be judged and the effectiveness of our management team determined by the degree to which the vision is shared. Corporations and companies today have visions, but they are rarely shared.

Next, our winning companies will possess sophisticated ways to acquire and integrate feedback, understanding that the value equation has changed. We and our companies will be good listeners and will pay attention to all information sources: customers, employees, competitors, educators, and politicians. Most important, however, our information-leveraged companies will drive technology and establish multiple mechanisms to collect, process, and use information provided by information clearing houses. Two major types of clearing houses will dominate: those focused on collecting information externally and those focused on linking information internally.

Fourth, our information-age companies will be composed of professionals who are accountable, skilled, and knowledgeable in the ways of using feedback to drive information and get the most from their people. Managers will be capable of doing their own analysis, and they will be expected to act on it within the scope of the shared vision. Real empowerment will be a fact. Who we know will be subordinated to "what" we know. Merit will once again be a primary requisite for advancement and promotion.

We as business leaders will be required to be disciplined, caring, and tough. We will make sure that our people are trained, cared for, rewarded, and able to execute the actions necessary to make the company vision a reality. We will be capable of managing systems, virtual teams and our own organizations simultaneously. We will be called *facilitators*. Partnership and output, skill and accountability, not manipulation and accommodation will be valued.

Next, our 21st century companies will be more organic than structural. We will act a lot more like the school of fish I saw, leveraging the human capabilities of our people who work within our companies, rather than the hierarchical, stovepipe-driven mechanistic bureaucracies of the waning industrial age. Strange! Human beings have visions and operate to fulfill them. We collect feedback from multiple internal and external sources. We share and use information that is collected analyzed and distributed from information clearing houses (the brain) in our bodies without regard for its source. We do all this for the sake of achieving balance and order, so we are in control and succeed. What is keeping us from doing the same in our businesses?

For companies, the organic analog, of course, is technology. Once we take control of it, rather than letting it control us, we will be on our way. Control will give way to form, function, output, and market domination. Information will be valued for what it adds rather than for where it comes from. Planning information, marketing information, financial information will lose their stovepipe limitations and uniqueness. Planners will be empowered because they can truly focus on making the shared vision a reality rather than fighting never-ending political information battles.

Finally, our companies will truly appreciate the value of information. They will understand that the quicker they can acquire and drive information, the lower will be their operating costs. This has always been an operational imperative, but the technology we now have makes it a decisive profit driver in the business world for the first time.

With timely information, a business's products will be more competitive and their operations more responsive. A number of studies point out a number of truths that now will be within the reach and control of companies that master the art of driving information: 1) for every increase in top ratings of customer satisfaction, the greater the repurchase, recommendations, and loyalty of customers; 2) for every increase in performance-related employee satisfaction the lower the training costs, turnover, and absenteeism of the workforce. All this directly translates to improved profits, making information the profit driver of the 21st century. The one who drives the information wins the game!

Get the picture? If you are still skeptical, I can't blame you, given that business professionals have been trained to focus on "what is" rather than "what might be." Further, we like to see something work before we sign on. OK, fair enough! Let's take the first step in our seven direct steps to market domination and turn to a more detailed discussion of the battle within.

CHAPTER I
Information Game Summary

Let the Game Begin

Remember
- It's not change, it's a revolution.
- Winning the information game requires that we drive information rather than letting it drive us.
- The need is balance and order.
- The opportunity is insight and innovation.
- The goal of the seven steps is to create companies that leverage feedback, adapt, and drive information.
- Driving information to ensure organizational balance and sustainment results in business domination, improved profits, and success.

CHAPTER II

WIN THE BATTLE WITHIN

*"Habit is habit, and not to be
flung out of the window by
any man, but coaxed downstairs
a step at a time."*
—Mark Twain

There is a growing realization that all the technology in the world will not give us the tools to win in the marketplace. To survive and learn how to drive information we must first come to grips with those personal, internal forces that drive our habits and can get in the way of using business feedback effectively. Alas, it almost seems we have been misled. Technology was supposed to raise us above and insulate us from such sticky problems. But the simple fact is that we cannot ignore our inner longings and fears any longer as drivers of good or bad business behavior.

When we think about it, there is really nothing new about the requirement to look inward. The problem is that, as a standard business practice, many of us have forgotten how to do it or we don't want to. These days it's as if it's up to someone else to prove that the need to change is greater than the comfort of staying the

Winning the Information Game

same. "I'm OK regardless of the feedback, and by the way, I'm not going to listen anyway!"

I was sitting in a long, seemingly endless meeting when the senior chairing the meeting started critiquing the slides being used by the presenter instead of listening to the presentation. The topic was fairly important to the company's on-going business operations, but it seemed like the senior had tuned everything out from the start. Maybe it was because the proposal to fix things required a number of changes that would directly impact the senior's operation. The presenter never did get to the bottom line because, at that point, others on the senior's staff started picking at the briefing and the presenter left in full retreat. I had witnessed another victory for the status quo.

In spite of such counterproductive behavior, the challenge of learning and changing is wrapped up in letting go of the old and embracing the new. It almost always involves personal risk, and we must be willing to reach out. To do this, it is important that our internal barriers to using feedback and becoming information drivers be faced first. Unless we free ourselves inside, how can we creatively talk about things like hardware, business strategies, tactics and techniques of moving to successful information-age ways of acquiring, processing, and using information? You can't drive into the future by looking in the rearview mirror!

More pragmatically, however, by facing our internal barriers first, at least when we ignore the feedback that suggests the need to change, we do so knowing our personal reasons for doing so. Then we can avoid falling victim to much of the contradictory business behavior we see today. For some, this is a tall order.

Take the story of the young business professional who arrived at the pearly gates after an unfortunate accident. Saint Peter, feeling sorry for her, offered her a chance to get some feedback before making a choice. "You will be allowed to check out both heaven and hell and then make a choice," he said. On checking out heaven she frankly found the place a little dull. In contrast, when she visited hell, the locals wined and dined her like there was no tomorrow. On returning to the pearly gates she told Saint Peter she had decided to go to hell. When she arrived there for the second time the place looked more like a steaming dump than the sparkling banquet hall she remembered. She asked the devil what had happened. He replied, "Before, we were recruiting you! Now you're staff!"

THE INTERNAL BATTLES

There is another important reason for dealing with our internal battles first. The barriers they promote are much more active today because they are being influenced by the fact that we are living through the death struggle of one type of business system—the hierarchical, stovepipe, control-driven, managerial-heavy organization and the emergence of another—the information-leveraged and engineered, adaptive business. And the resulting internal fear and confusion can blind us to dangers that can threaten our business.

Change never comes without a cost. Ask those who from their blacksmith shops watched the arrival of the horseless carriage (the automobile) a century or so ago. Or, if you wish, visualize how Pony Express riders must have felt as they watched telegraph wires being strung across the West or watched the joining of our country by rail in 1869 at Promontory Point, Utah. Or if you prefer military disasters, relive the days in 1940 when the French and English behind the supposedly impenetrable Maginot Line were trampled underfoot as Hitler's *Blitzkrieg* swept the remnants of their armies into the English Channel.

To begin to make information our servant and adapt to the information age revolution, companies, and, more specifically, managers and leaders must battle to overcome three sets of internal feedback barriers.

1. The Technological Battle. Business professionals must stop thinking about technology in a defensive manner and begin to leverage its feedback potential. Our ambivalence is killing our competitiveness and making too many consultants far too rich. Such behavior makes me want to yell, "Get out of the defensive crouch and attack!" Businesses, regardless of their physical location in the world, have an increasing capacity to compete because of technology. It is no longer possible for a company to rest easy, thinking that it can insulate its employees and their products from the competition. Physical and political barriers cannot protect a business from increasingly tough competition that knows no time, spatial, or electronic limitations.

As if to confirm this point, in her compelling book *The Death of Distance*, author Frances Cairncross warns that technology is destroying all physical barriers. She points out very clearly that she believes the next twenty-five years will see a total reformation of social relationships, governmental practices, and business operations. Interestingly, even though the origins are in technology, she characterizes outcomes as being "about opportunity and about increasing human contact." And she suggests that it will be easier than ever for people with initiative and ideas to turn them into business ventures.

Looking at things in more detail, thanks to the unprecedented electronic developments of the past quarter of a century, the emerging reality is that business professionals have to be consummate users of information designed to enhance customer dialogue and product competitiveness. There is no choice! Those of us who want to compete must overcome our internal reluctance, reach out, and learn how to leverage technology.

We can't delegate the responsibility to leverage technology to someone like a computer programmer just because we don't feel comfortable. Electronics are busy busting all paradigms, driving hierarchical organizations into extinction, and there is no going back. Do you remember the days in the early 1970s when a calculator that could only add, subtract, multiply and divide cost over $100 at Sears and Roebuck. Where are we today? What happened to Sears? What happened to that calculator?

The information age is increasingly characterized by digital electronic pathways that radiate out in every direction. Instantaneous information access is available for all that want or need it. Reduction of time-distance barriers to the speed of light is a fact. Unfortunately, the personal internal defense of professional denial is active, and our behavior has been much slower to adapt.

I remember very vividly an encounter with a senior manager of a retail business regarding information he was getting about his employees and customers. He had a problem and wanted it fixed immediately. He had been insulated for so long by his staff that only the good information was getting to him. When technology began to overwhelm the existing filtering systems and he began to see some of the negative information, his reaction was predictable. He felt that all this new information was the fault of the system and those who ran it, and he wanted things fixed. The information just couldn't be that negative!

The lesson is that while information processing, storing, and transmitting systems have infiltrated our companies, they have done so with predictably contradictory results. Unfortunately, they come face-to-face with our existing Byzantine bureaucracies and rigid managerial styles which seek to control rather than enable. On the positive side, managers who try to control feedback flow and tone are discovering that this activity is a losing cause. Still, a manager reported to me recently that his company had discovered that its Intranet was so popular as a communications tool that it was interfering with established operational control systems to the consternation of those trying to control the information flow. The answer? They shut down the Intranet!

We have been captives of our internal technological insecurity so long, that the business press has had a field day of late. It has been making light of the fact that numerous blue chip companies have embraced the idea of Internet email, only to be flooded with messages they could neither handle nor act on because of their out-of-synch internal operations and processes.

In another company, I encountered several frustrated managers who tried to change the units to which their employees were assigned in their department by submitting a single list in one email message. They were informed that this wouldn't do. The technician told them that the information would have to be submitted separately on each employee as it was easier to enter into the computer. Guess who ended up in charge?

Or how many of us have ever watched someone or been guilty ourselves of hand writing a memo and then having our secretary or executive assistant keystroke it into an email message and transmit it in our name? If you haven't, then you probably haven't visited a corporate headquarters lately. Or what about the computer that sits on the desk, never to be used by our colleagues? Funnier and sadder still, how many of us know someone who carries a laptop on trips and never uses it?

The only saving grace is that such foolishness won't last because these sorts of activities can't survive. In effect, there is a new disciplinarian on the block—it's technology and it is changing the business feedback equation. The problem today isn't the lack of feedback. It's the lack of our ability to manage, assimilate and use it. If we and our companies try to control everything, competing data and political battles can and do dominate business deliberations. The outcome is companies who are choking on increasing volumes of feedback and are dying.

I've witnessed the sad process many times when organizations attempt to remedy the problem by applying old practices and procedures and engineering the new technology to serve and sustain the old business behavior. Instead of trying to identify the other "burning platforms" and potential business problems, we ought to look inward and see if our own platform is on fire.

Interestingly, within our increasingly information-rich world, the only people who appear capable of adapting so far are our customers. They are winning the technological battle because they are not encumbered by or caught up with the bureaucracy of much of modern business. Customers rightly recognize that the power of the electronic age is to be found in an ability to use the feedback it provides to extend themselves beyond their physical surroundings, enhancing their ability to get what they want.

Unlike their business brethren, chastised in a *Wall Street Journal* article by Brett Battles and David Mark entitled "Companies that Just Don't Get IT" (Information Technology) for their failure to manage Information Technology and letting themselves be managed, customers aren't afraid to take charge. In sum, customers recognize that information can't be controlled, but it can be facilitated, used and leveraged. If there is any one truth of the new information age practices and a key to winning the internal technological battle this is it. The new knowledge worker professional envisioned by Michael Hammer in his book *Beyond Reengineering* is already here, but unfortunately for a lot of companies they have arrived in the person of the customer.

For example, over the past decade, to the consternation of sales people everywhere, customers have learned to leverage telephone technology. Electronic telephone developments such as Caller ID and answering machines are used to control telemarketing as well as other telephonic intrusions. In other parts of our electronic world, customer email bulletin boards increasingly are the places where products and services are being discussed and profits and losses determined. "Word of mouth!" is taking on a whole new meaning. Just visit a "chat" room on the Internet sometime. In the process, junk mail is finding its resting place in trash cans much more quickly.

Now customers can even get their hands on a free piece of software from the web called "Third Voice." It allows them to post their comments on a company's web pages whether the owner of that Web site wants it or not. Only those with the software can read the comments, but the reactions of fury from businesses and the owners of Web sites have been predictable. It remains to be seen if the software survives, but it does make the point about who is in charge!

Finally, customers are making networking and partnering increasingly important concepts. Isn't it ironic? When we become customers looking for feedback, we seem to understand and are interested in what technology can do for us. When we put on our business hats and become corporate, our brains seem to turn to hamburger, and we forget we're in charge and have a right to drive things.

Technology has given us the capability to move into the information age. Customers are defining the knowledge principles and are leading the way in determining its emerging form and content. Unless we are willing to face our own reluctance and master the technology we have created, we will continue to flounder.

2. *The Operational Battle.* Turning to the operational battle within, we are still primarily driven by externally developed, managed and controlled policies, procedures and templates in our companies. They serve to limit the operational options that we can use. Show me the executive who rigidly adheres to the operational plan to know what to do, and I will show you a company who is at risk. In a world increasingly characterized by speed and fluidity of action, such approaches almost guarantee failure. Ken Shelton captures the essence of this problem in his book *Beyond Counterfeit Leadership,* in which he characterizes the dominant business leadership model of today as being like the plantation leadership of the 18th and 19th centuries. He finds the business world full of overseers and foremen, masquerading as vice presidents and other company officers. All are dedicated to controlling things and keeping the workers in line rather than building the business.

To win the operational battle, our thinking needs to focus on developing implicit, internally driven operational practices instead of relying on external structure, rigidity, and templates. This allows us to take advantage of all feedback that may come our way and initiate immediate action to keep things moving forward.

Our objective must be to develop operationally flexible employees and managers capable of "reading' their environment and partnering with their customers and other employees. The business literature today is replete with marvelous examples of what happens when we demonstrate operational flexibility, but I will always remember the words of one customer: "You took care of me when I needed help and gave me the benefit of the doubt. Now I'm going to buy my wife one of your products just because I know you will take care of her too."

Clear business vision, coherent, self-directed performance, and an enlightened but superbly disciplined work force that responds on the basis of implicit guidance is the answer to the operational business challenge. Some things never change, you say! What about empowerment? What about participative management?

Without internal discipline and an implicit framework, such concepts represent at best a gross misuse of feedback that results in employee manipulation and appeasement on our part. At worst, they constitute an ineffective, chaotic strategy that lacks any coherent, internally sustained direction or motivation. In the information age, externally driven practices will lead to environments characterized by envy and self-interest that slowly destroy us internally and render our companies ineffective.

Perhaps most telling is the fact that without internally sustained operational imperatives, trained and sustained through technology, we and our companies will be too slow to survive in the fast moving, fluid information age. Here feedback and its rapid conversion to information useable by everyone provides the keys to success.

The information age demands that we develop operational feedback practices and thinking that are proactive not reactive (see Appendix A). Further, they must be creative and motivating, not restrictive and limiting. In short, for us to win the internal operational struggle we need to become electronically connected to our customers—to become their biological extensions. Let me explain this with an analogy.

Biologically, we are feedback-driven, adaptive organisms that seek balance and the satisfaction of our needs. We collect and turn the feedback into information that we use to achieve our aims and goals. Given technological and operational advances, couldn't our businesses be designed and operated similarly?

Internally, our nervous system serves to transmit feedback, some to be put into action immediately and other feedback to be evaluated, stored, discarded or used to learn. Moreover, feedback sources are both external and internal. Further, our nervous system is linked through a number of processing centers or "information clearing houses," the most complex being the brain. Here is where things are analyzed and converted into information, which is then shared to promote action. The whole process is geared to speed and adaptation, which emphasize action first and counting and analyzing second.

In like manner, because of technology we and our businesses now have the opportunity to position ourselves operationally to become electronic mirrors of our customers, in the process building the basis for a true partnership with those who consume and use our products and services. Organizationally, operations truly have the opportunity to follow function. So what's the problem? It's certainly not outside! Could it be our attitudes?

3. The Attitudinal Battle. Another internal battle that we must confront is our own prior learning and established attitudes. I frequently ask audiences the following question: What's wrong with the following information-processing order: count, analyze, fix? I tell them that during the industrial age when things moved at a relatively slow pace, nothing was wrong. In the information age when things move at nearly the speed of light, everything is wrong. By the time one counts, analyzes, and recommends a fix, the fix is obsolete. The new order needs to be fix, count, and analyze continuously and simultaneously. Only in this way can we hope to leverage information, remain relevant, and be flexible enough to change our attitudinal frameworks. Bill Gates rightly warns in the introduction to his book *Business @ the Speed of Thought:* "Though at heart most business problems are information problems, almost no one is using information well."

But this is a relatively minor attitudinal battle. Much more serious battles involve matters of organizational influence, politics, control, and power. When you think about it, one of the industrial-age hierarchical organization's defining reasons for existence was to exercise power, whether it was over a product, or over others—once again the vision of Ken Shelton's plantation leadership. What happens when the variables that we historically have used to define power, specifically information, are no longer controllable or under the control of those who grew up in hierarchical organizations? We have a real attitudinal problem. To operate in the information age, business professionals are going to have to come to grips with this internal battle.

Every time we are charged with creating something new in our companies or building new business teams, we are sure to find that at least one of the battles that must be fought has to do with attitudes—those within the changing organization and those outside resisting its growth. Most commonly the cause is fear. Fear of the unknown. Fear of loss of influence. Just plain fear or anxiety. The attitudes that follow all act to destroy an important business glue—trust. Who do you talk to? Who do you trust? The authors of the book *Working Knowledge,* published by the Harvard Business Press, consider trust so important to effective business knowledge sharing that they characterize it as the critical element to company knowledge management and success.

One of my favorite illustrations to explain the issue of internal attitudes and trust has to do with the requirement to share information to succeed in today's electronic world. The departmental manager I was talking to at his company headquarters couldn't understand why he had to share information about his operations with others in the company. When he settled down, he agreed to share only if he knew who would get the information. What he didn't realize was that his attitudes blinded him to the fact that information age operations within our companies demand just the opposite. The problem is not who has information, but rather who doesn't have it. The people with whom the manager wasn't sharing information were just the people who might need it to make a quick decision and keep the business from failing.

So the task is clear! To use feedback to drive information, we must win the technological, operational and attitudinal battles within ourselves. By so doing, we will gain the will and the courage to start leveraging and managing technology to change our operational habits and modify our business attitudes. Once this happens, the result will be a new awareness of overlooked business opportunities and renewed excitement for business innovation.

Most important, we may avoid making comments like the one made in 1957 by an editor in charge of business books at Prentice Hall: "I have traveled the length and breadth of this country, and talked with the best people, and I can assure you that data processing is a fad that won't last out the year." With the battle within as the base, let us now move on to consider Step two: Sharing the business vision.

CHAPTER II

INFORMATION GAME SUMMARY

Step I: Win the Battle Within

Change the way you view information to
- Win the technological battle by deciding to take charge of technology and make it work for you.
- Win the operational battle by changing your behavior to be more implicit and responsive, designed to enable and empower.
- Win the attitudinal battle that drives your personal and corporate behavior by remaining open and willing to see new and different views.

The battles are critical because
- Technology has changed the business equation forever, from count, analyze, fix, to fix, count, and analyze continuously and simultaneously.
- Rigidity is out, fluidity is in.
- Constant change is not sustainable but adaptability is.
- Technology is the new disciplinarian.
- Customers are in charge.
- Information can't be controlled but it can be facilitated.
- Proactive not reactive thinking promotes business success.
- External control is out, implicit action is in.

CHAPTER III
SHARE THE BUSINESS VISION

"People only see what they are prepared to see."
—*Ralph Waldo Emerson*

Step two requires that we share the business vision. It is one thing for us to understand and successfully confront the internal battles required to develop the behaviors needed to use feedback so that we can drive information. It is quite another to establish an effective framework to sustain personal business changes and any new business activity that follows. For the question is: How do we manage technology, harness the collective energy of our people, and connect all those electronic cables in our companies while sustaining the entire effort?

The answer to the question, with a couple of twists, is really not very new. Rather, it depends on renewed application of an enduring, unifying concept. Succeeding and becoming effective information-drivers depends more than ever on everyone in the business having a well-founded and shared business vision. And when you see the output in action, there is no question about the value of vision in driving information.

In this regard, a number of the thoughts in this chapter build on the three years I spent researching and writing an operations manual on "Leadership and Command at Senior levels," for the United States Army. It was a unique, absolutely absorbing experience that brought me into contact with the Army's most senior active duty and retired professionals, individuals who have had to exercise their management and leadership skills under extreme conditions few of us in business ever face. The research and writing effort demonstrated to me clearly the importance and power of a shared vision to any important activity. It becomes even more critical when the speed of information flow continues to increase.

WHAT EXACTLY IS A SHARED VISION?

All personal and collective action starts with a vision. An example of an enduring vision for all Americans is embodied in the Declaration of Independence. Today it still stands as the most basic statement of what must be shared if Americans are to maintain their unity. Building on this vision, for those of us in the business world, is a shared idea of what our companies must be capable of doing by some future point in time. It is the target and source of our business balance, allowing us to meet and dominate our competitors with a team that has internalized what is required and is motivated to achieve the desired result.

A vision is not a mission statement plastered on some corporate wall or some abstract and useless statement of hoped for results. IT MUST BE UNDERSTOOD, REAL, AND SHARED FROM THE CEO DOWN TO THE LAST WORKER ON THE FRONT LINE. The higher you go in businesses with good shared visions, the more you see executives taking the lead to make it happen. What does our company need to accomplish today, tomorrow, or one year from now to achieve the desired result? How is our company developed, structured, and sustained to achieve that capability? What can I do to help?

A fundamental task for successful businesses involves bringing resources to bear in order to beat and stay ahead of the competition. Effort is applied most effectively when the managers and leaders of our companies, in advance of events, establish the conditions we want to obtain at the conclusion of a business activity.

Share the Business Vision

Here I'm referring to anything from a sales campaign to a new product development effort.

Only when we understand and internalize the ends we seek can we prepare and communicate to our employees clear guidance and direction from which flow the concepts and actions needed to ensure success. Further, once we know where we want to go, we can decide what feedback will be needed to drive the information we use and move us toward our goal. No successful business venture is possible without a clear vision of how it should conclude.

Lots of historical examples illustrate this aspect of vision. My favorite, however, is a current example. It is obvious now that AT&T wireless had launched a 1998 campaign to change the way we all look at cell phones and set a mark on the wall for its entire operation at the same time. The television, radio, and print ads blare out that you can make calls using a cellular phone which are, within the calling plan time limits, considered local calls anywhere in the United States. The ads end with a comment to the effect—"This might be the only phone you will ever need." So what's the vision? For the business it is to have the cell phone replace wired phones. How? Get the customer to buy the new cell phone and the program. The end is clear and its unifying force is very visible from the CEO to the sales force. If the vision is shared then effective execution can follow.

I know this because when I went into an AT&T wireless store to consider buying into the program, I experienced effective shared vision at work. The customer contact person not only reinforced what I had heard on television, but displayed an ability to enlarge on the theme so effectively that I bought in without hesitation and left the store with a top-of-the line phone, fully programmed and ready to go. More than that, subsequently, the salesperson followed up to see how I was doing with the phone, even offering helpful hints on how to use the phone more effectively. Now that's service! Now that's shared vision helping to make it happen! And they must be succeeding because the whining in the communications world about the fact that "Ma Bell" is back has been growing.

CHARACTERISTICS OF A SHARED VISION

1. Provides a unified reference point. A company's shared vision serves as a source of effectiveness and shared focus. For CEOs it is the "reservoir of energy which ignites their will." For the rest of us, it is that sense of certainty that provides humanistic direction to otherwise uncertain efforts. Within our businesses it can be an intuitive sensing by the CEO, a precise directive from one of our seniors, or a manager's intent for a sales effort or departmental change. Regardless of where it originates, for our businesses to succeed, there can be only one vision, because it is the reference point against which we measure progress. In fact, when properly formed, it provides its own capability to change or affirm its direction by the way it serves to drive the collection of feedback and the use of the resulting information.

2. Provides the capability to organize because it establishes focus for our actions and guidance to our companies. All too often, guidance can have no force of certainty other than the personality of the one ordering action. When this is so, no sense of direction is sustainable. Moreover, shared vision is the basis from which the CEO and the rest of us generate the moral and ethical leadership power required to activate the internal professional and personal resources of our employees. It is the source of an effective business culture tied to the bottom line. This, in turn, musters and sustains team trust, cohesion, commitment, and the will to meet any competitive challenge.

3. Aids management in developing the necessary employee skills and competencies. The leaders of a company form the broad framework within which all feedback collection and information sharing at all lower levels is developed, nurtured, practiced, and sustained. In turn, their effectiveness is based on perspectives and skills that require highly developed competency, character, steadfastness, and boldness. Anything less is nothing more than glorified self-interest. Unless those in leadership positions have a well-developed and shared sense of things which grows from and is in harmony with the shared vision of what their responsibilities entail, developing the desired actions in their businesses will be difficult if not impossible to attain.

4. Focuses effort and defines what must be "known. "A properly shared business vision focuses our employees and our resources in ways which ensure that all of us are actors whose total effort is greater than the sum of the individual parts. Not all companies are succeeding, because I came across a number of blurbs on the Internet, some of which read, "99 percent of lawyers give the rest a bad name!" "I feel like I'm diagonally parked in a parallel universe!" or "The sooner you fall behind the more time you'll have to catch up!"

On a more serious note, the manager I was talking with was perplexed by the absenteeism in his operating division. Don't "they" know that even with automation we can't produce the product without a full and experienced team available? When we have to move people and tasks around, it messes things up. When we looked into the problem we found that the employees thought that the vision was "success through automation" and not "success through people with better automation." They had concluded that they really didn't matter. When that erroneous view got corrected, things straightened out in a hurry. To that point, because of the incorrect vision focus, employees had stopped communicating, and the feedback needed to fix things had gotten disconnected and lost. To make matters worse, the manager was no longer in a position to drive information.

EFFECTIVE SHARED BUSINESS VISION ACTIVITIES

Three activities on our part are critical to establishing effective shared business visions. Because without a means to focus effort and direct action, it is impossible for us to drive information and sustain the team effort required to succeed in the highly competitive information age. All of us in management and leadership positions need to ensure that we provide the necessary purpose, direction, and motivation. We know that without implementing guideposts, operational and departmental focus is impossible to maintain. We also never forget that our first responsibility is to ensure that the vision framework is shared. That is how we as the leadership add value and ensure consistent movement toward the desired goal.

1. Purpose. Establishing purpose provides our businesses and our employees with a reason to achieve and sacrifice. It is a known fact that employees do best when they know why they are doing something. Collectively, knowing "why" we are doing something gives our work and effort meaning. Unfortunately, in the industrial-age organizations that still dot the landscape, sharing information and insights is the last thing the leadership considers. Yet it is the key to our success in the information age.

Establishing purpose depends heavily on our collective ability to understand what is required of our businesses. Further, it is based on an appreciation of the strategic, operational, and tactical goals of our businesses. Hiding such information until we get into our boardrooms can no longer be allowed. Finally, and most important, purpose depends on a well-formed ability of all levels of our company management and leadership to communicate vision-based business intentions clearly so that we link the larger business aims to our company's long- and short-term goals.

However we arrive at our shared understanding of the business vision, as effective company leaders and managers, we must pass on to our employees a coherent picture of how our departments or units fit into the "big picture." When we do this we impart a sense of priority and importance for the tasks that must be accomplished and relate how success or failure of our effort will impact our companies as a whole. Only in this way can there be any sense of empowerment, because effective actions to drive information always take place within a framework. Therefore, today's concepts of participative management without vision-based focus and established frameworks are recipes for disaster. Focus is always and will always be central to effective action.

In our businesses, events will not unfold as planned, assumptions may prove wrong, and assigned tasks may be inappropriate. Knowing the reasons for our company's actions helps us judge what new tasks might be more appropriate when such problems inevitably arise. Further, it leads to overall harmony in execution and effective use of resources when executing our company's strategies. Finally, it provides the means for independent thought and decisions to solve unanticipated problems that are best resolved when acted on rapidly. In short, it provides real empowerment.

A wonderful example of this sort of empowerment is reported to exist at Monarch Marking Systems in Miamisburg, Ohio. Here employees clearly understand the importance of action that supports the vision. No worker teams are allowed where teams dream up pie-in-the-sky solutions. Instead, based on a shared vision and operational focus, teams only work on improving specific operations deemed critical to the company's effective operation.

As was noted in *The Wall Street Journal*, teams at Monarch Marking Systems are charged with executing their own solutions, including working out necessary changes with other departments and vendors. To make matters tougher, the company also directs that teams are not to last beyond 30 days. The desired result is solutions that promote accomplishment of the shared vision in creative, practical ways without a lot of bureaucracy.

In the Monarch Marking Systems example, the payoff for shared vision-based business purpose is internalized employee focus. It enables everyone to operate in a disciplined manner, within the established scope of the vision. Further, it enables the company's leaders and mangers to trust their employees to use initiative to align their actions with the business vision in ways that cannot be forecast before the action. Finally, establishing purpose creates the conditions in which employees and units freely share an understanding of what needs to be done, and knowing they are trusted commit themselves to the company without reservation.

2. Direction. Our acts of providing direction dictate that all of us in leadership and management positions chart a clear and unambiguous course for our people, based on a shared vision, and create the conditions that allow our departments to succeed. Manipulation and appeasement are not part of the equation, because they generally arise from self-interest and personal ambition.

Winning the Information Game

The speed and fluidity of the information age demand that to establish appropriate direction, leaders and managers must set appropriate goals and standards, develop individuals and teams, ensure discipline, and train their people. It's hard work because it involves true business caring and nurturing. Further, it's work-based; and it's outcome-dependent. Goals and standards provide the azimuth. Individuals and teams provide the depth needed. Discipline provides the assurance that goals and standards are met in the absence of the boss. Finally, training provides the confidence to know that the desired results we want can be achieved.

As company leaders and managers we clearly state and assign tasks to our employees. In addition to such direct guidance, we also influence action indirectly. We promote values; set standards for task accomplishment; enforce discipline; establish operating procedures; ensure the training of our employees and units in the appropriate business methods, and techniques; and establish policies and regulations. Gone is the Human Resources watchdog. Unless such activities become everyone's internalized habits, our companies will not possess the flexibility to adapt to the demands of the information age.

When leaders and managers couple purpose with direction, they reinforce the capability to communicate their vision and intent, knowing what feedback is needed to drive things. Now not only do their employees know what must be done, they understand why it is necessary. Without purpose and direction in combination, no shared vision is complete, and communication of the needed guidance is problematic at best. Because companies are really people, the extent to which leaders and managers at all levels channel the separate wills and energies of the work force is the extent to which they unify effort and multiply the competitive power of their companies.

3. Motivation. Business motivation requires much more than providing a salary or a bonus. But one would not know this, given the preoccupation with monetary schemes in business today. Monetary motivation is a mirage. It is necessary but not sufficient for the success of our businesses. Therefore, if we are to be successful we must view motivation quite differently. We know it takes perseverance and force of will to succeed in a highly competitive world. We also know management is responsible for ensuring that the required motivation exists. And this is hard work because others cannot be manipulated into a sustained motivational posture.

To become successful, information-driving companies, we must motivate by developing the proper ethical perspective, sustaining a positive and progressive team climate, and fostering a sense of unity and information sharing that generates an unshakable business cohesion—no elitist, executive dining rooms or we-they mentalities allowed. In contrast, those of us at executive levels must operate from a premise that we are the keepers of the moral force that flows from good business values and sustains and engages the will of our employees to achieve business advantage over our competitors. In companies that possess these attributes, we will not hear all-too-common reactions to directives from the boss like, "I know that's what the memo says but that's not what the boss really means!" or "For every action there is an equal and opposite criticism."

As company leaders and managers we also must be technically and professionally competent to be able to motivate our people. Employees have a right to expect that their managers know what they are doing. Therefore, we build shared values and promote consistent ethical standards needed to create effective teams. Moreover, we are visible all the time and circulate among our people. No isolated executive offices in businesses with effective shared visions. No unnecessary barriers either; after all, the information age knows no such limits.

Finally, all of us who are company executives ensure that mutual trust and confidence are maintained between management and employees. Lack of trust across a business is the failure of seniors.

IMPLEMENTING THE SHARED VISION

When implementing a shared company vision, we as leaders and managers need to keep in mind two facts. First, our companies must be prepared to compete and succeed. They are business entities first and social organizations second. Without competitive success nothing else matters. Business operations are results-oriented activities, and the fluid nature of the emerging information age is placing an ever-increasing premium on company competence, cohesion and immediate, independent action. Therefore, improvisation, initiative, and assertiveness must be well-developed at all levels.

The inevitable question arises: How can we break the industrial age tendency to operate on the basis of feeding the dogs, riding the horses, and shooting the tigers? The answer is to be found in broadening our perspective. It's not that only one type of leader or worker is required, rather businesses need all types. It's not caring leaders or task-oriented leaders. It's not compassion or candor. It is both! If we see problems as either/or situations, we haven't grasped the essence of information-age business activity, and we won't be prepared to drive information.

Second, to be successful information-age companies that dominate our competitors, we must recognize that success depends on knowing what is possible. That depends on clearing all impediments from the acquisition of timely, reliable feedback-driven information that enables implementation of the shared vision. Good information, widely shared and used, is the beginning and the end for competitive success. This enables our companies to balance competing business demands with the reality of the situation they confront. Of course, the presumption is that leaders and managers are attitudinally prepared and possess the required business skills.

Effective vision-based companies value information and leadership competency, using both to leverage the multiple talents of all employees. The word "and" rather than the words "either/or" are most commonly used. It's individuals *and* teams, not individuals or teams. It's standards *and* compassion, not either standards or compassion. And it's leaders *and* managers, not leaders or managers.

Company characteristics include shared vision and values; numerous high-performing teams integrated into sophisticated information processing and distribution networks that operate independently within the established vision; common information standards and requirements; open, aggressive pursuit of feedback;

Share the Business Vision

an instantaneous ability to anticipate and deal with the unexpected; and a shared understanding of competitors and customers.

With the concept of shared vision now in focus, let us turn to the matter of solving the riddle posed by the requirement to deal with the matters of interactivity, integration and information.

CHAPTER III

INFORMATION GAME SUMMARY

Step II: See, understand, and promote a shared business vision

- Business vision is a shared concept of what the company and its people must be able to do to succeed by some future point.

A shared vision can:
- Be the source of the company's will.
- Establish an ethical framework.
- Provide a reference point against which progress is measured.
- Focus business activity

Three activities are critical to establishing shared vision:
- Establishing purpose.
- Providing direction.
- Motivating the company. Implementing a shared vision is a matter of ensuring balance and sustaining activity, never losing sight of the goal by knowing what is possible.
- Living the vision.
- Implementing the vision so that everyone thinks "and," not "either/or."

CHAPTER IV

SOLVE THE RIDDLE OF THE THREE I'S

"Everything should be made as simple as possible, but not simpler."
—*Albert Einstein*

Step three to winning the information game and achieving market domination demands that we solve the riddle of the three I's. Taking steps to win the battle within and having a shared vision that focuses us on our business target certainly can help us win the information game. Collectively they will also allow us to start leveraging and driving information. However, ultimate success is not just a matter of internal issues or a firm view of where we need to go. We must consider and confront three external factors. What do these three failed business situations have in common? The situations are real. Only the names of the people and companies have been changed to protect resumes and reputations. After all, as the saying goes, "No one is listening until you make a mistake!"

THE FAILURES

Case 1: The wrong way to interact. Thanks to the efforts of an innovative and very active product development department, the mail order company's marketing group was presented with an unprecedented opportunity to get to market first with a wonderful new product. Success would have meant a major positive impact on the bottom line. All they had to do was connect with their customers and handle their responses.

The background work in the company had been well integrated. Further, the information on the target market provided by the research group was excellent. The product launch was intended to target customers seeking to maintain their youth and vitality—pre-boomers over 60. In their enthusiasm, the young, energetic marketing group members made some assumptions to speed things up. The target group liked news magazines. Moreover, they were generally affluent. So the decision was made to use a print sales campaign. Since they figured they were dealing with a pretty sophisticated market, they turned their creative advertisers loose, telling them to come up with mailing pieces that would "knock the customers' socks off!"

Selecting a print campaign did limit things a bit, but the marketing group felt they had defined the target correctly. What they were really proud of, however, was the fact that using their new advertising support capabilities would simplify and speed things up considerably. The print campaign seemed to begin promisingly. But after three months of frustration, complaints, and outright customer hostility to follow up on the marketing pieces, where they actually saw their customer satisfaction ratings go down, the marketing group declared the product launch a failure.

The analysis revealed that although they had had the right information on who would be interested in the product, the company never did connect. No sense of interactivity was ever established. The customers who were print-driven, as it turned out, were also a group that couldn't see well, didn't like fancy advertising, and were very traditional in their view of the world. They weren't ever going to respond to some slick campaign they couldn't read, much less understand given all of the graphics. Further, the customers were disappointed in the company for resorting to such gimmicks.

Solve the Riddle of Three I's

Case 2: Lack of integration. Let's shift our attention to the marketing offices of a subsidiary company of a large enterprise known for its "rock solid" insurance products. The marketing officer was looking over the results of some excellent general market research information that suggested opportunities to expand their sales to customers who owned multiple products with the parent company. Our marketer wondered if anyone at Corporate knew who these customers might be. If they did, the subsidiary could then certainly leverage the multiple customer access channels available to connect and take advantage of the market research.

When our marketer asked Corporate for the information, they politely replied that such information was not available. Not to be deterred, the marketer called several of the other subsidiary companies and was horrified to discover that there was no common way to determine which customers owned multiple products with the company. Consequently, the marketer gave up, and a wonderful marketing opportunity was lost. Reflection suggests that the integration of information was lacking. As a consequence, despite good information and good ways to connect with customers, no competitive advantage was realized.

Case 3: The case of the wrong information. In the corporate offices of another Fortune 500 company, the CEO's strategic planner was faced with a dilemma. Should the company's plans place priority on improving its customer service delivery through better use of technology or should it focus on providing more products on store shelves. The overall goal of the effort was to improve the company's bottom line, but both options carried major resource implications.

Analysis had suggested that customer access and interactivity were not a problem. Further, within the company, the product delivery and order fulfillment groups were well known for their ability to take and integrate things quite well for competitive advantage. However, when the call went out for information from which the CEO could make an executive decision, our planner discovered that it didn't exist.

What was provided was all sorts of data on inventory levels, cash register volumes, and the number of customers serviced by store, by time of day. Consequently, our planner had to take the data available and then convert it into information on which to base a recommendation to the CEO. The result was inconclusive information on which to base a recommendation regarding the available options. As a result, the decision was made to adopt the course of action which had the least resource impact. Not surprisingly, money was spent and the bottom line did not improve.

Our planner has since corrected the situation, but the lost competitive advantage, not to mention wasted resources, was significant. He knew he could integrate information and make it happen. And he knew he was on a firm interactive footing with the firm's customers. But without the right information at the right time, the company was unable to gain a competitive advantage.

THE RIDDLE

So just what do these three situations have in common? The answer should now be clear. Interactivity, integration, and information are three interrelated, continuous, and simultaneous external information-age activities that we must consider and deal with if we are to make information work for our companies. Overlook one of the three, and business failure can follow quickly. I call the problem the riddle of the Three I's.

The riddle poses the following question: How do we develop the organizational processes and capabilities required to deal with the simultaneous information age impact of INTERACTIVITY, INTEGRATION, and INFORMATION? Assuming that we are keeping our eyes firmly fixed on our customers and products, those of us who solve the riddle will increase the likelihood that we will be the business winners. Let's look at the three I's closer with a view to solving the riddle and drawing out what needs to be done to acquire, process, and use feedback better.

Solve the Riddle of Three I's

INTERACTIVITY

Interactivity is best viewed as a potential. It refers to the ways customers can interact with our companies and we with them. It used to be that the primary interaction choices were face-to-face and sometimes phone or mail. Boy, were those the good old days. As the following chart suggests, today there are at least nine different ways customers and companies can do business: phone, face-to-face, email, mail, fax, TV, kiosk, agent, and the Internet directly.

What does this mean? Do we sit around and wait for one of the communications channels to win the information game for us? No one channel has succeeded so far! What it means is that we'd better be ready to operate in all mediums because, theoretically, a transaction could start through an agent. Then the transaction could be continued by online email, fax, kiosk, TV, mail or phone. Finally, it could conclude through any one of these same access channels. And, as the arrival of virtual grocery stores like PeaPod suggest, retailers and grocery stores are not immune either. Add to the challenge the possibility that a customer may want to be able to do business seven days a week, twenty-four hours a day, and we really have a complex situation on our hands.

The day has arrived when customers can do business wherever, whenever, and however they want. The only saving grace is that very few customers will ever be so eclectic that they have no preferred ways of communicating and of doing business. Just as we as individuals have differing needs, our customers also have differing ways of interacting and going about doing business with us. This emerging reality is so important that some businesses are now beginning to segment their markets based on communications preferences.

Herein lies the solution to the matter of effectively connecting with and serving customers. We must know our customers so well that we understand and are able to respond using their preferred means of interaction. Demographics help, but knowing their behaviors and preferences is critical in the information age. Notice that the operative word is THEIR!

Winning the Information Game

In the quest to communicate and interact effectively with our customers, the first question we ought to ask is how do they like to do it? The medium is truly the "message," as was noted a number of years ago. Are they virtual customers? If so, then some interactive media approach is indicated. Do they prefer to read it? Then some print method is indicated. Or do they like to talk with a person? If so, then schedule a meeting or get up close and personal.

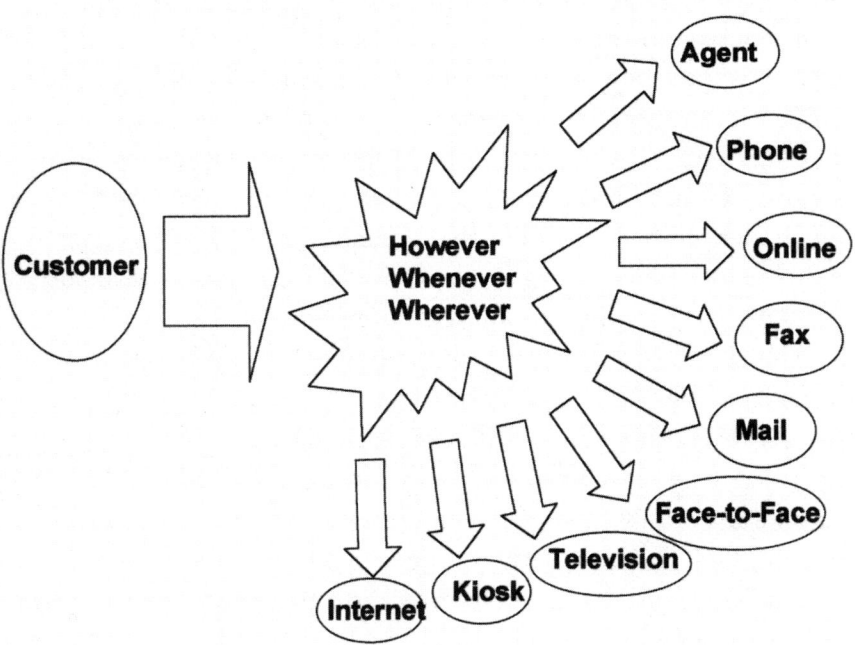

Broadening this approach a bit, if we know our customers' preferred modes of doing business, we can then position our interactive business capabilities accordingly, saving time, money, and aggravation for both parties. Hindsight suggests that some of

Solve the Riddle of Three I's

these points about interaction preferences could have been applied to the case where older customers were hit with print advertising they could neither read nor liked much. What about simpler designs? Bigger print? What about using a different medium, such as the telephone or TV? What about finding out what kind of communications they preferred in advance of events? Or finally, what about having ways to know more quickly whether or not the method of interaction was working?

We encountered a similar problem while I was at USAA that illustrates the need for responsiveness regardless of the method of interaction. Long-term customers were not responding to a request for their preferences on an insurance matter. When USAA investigated, it discovered that the group members were older, were not particularly technology literate, and had hearing problems, yet they were being asked to respond through use of a telephone voice response prompter. When the telephone prompter was replaced with real people, the problem was solved.

The lesson, and one reality of effective leveraging of information age technology, is to make sure there are enough interactive choices so that customers can pick their preferred mode of interaction. Better yet, make sure we know their preferences in advance. It is a truism today that homogeneity of interaction has been replaced with diversity of interaction.

For example, contrary to the fondest wishes of technophiles like myself and others who hype the computer-driven Internet as the only interactive choice for the future, it is just not going to happen. Again, economist Frances Cairncross captures the issue in her book *The Death of Distance*. She suggests that the Internet will simply take its place as just another means of interaction and communication. It will never dominate any more than the telephone did over mail when they were the only forms of long-range communication. Each found its niche. In fact, there are even those bold enough to suggest the computer as a distinct machine could ultimately become invisible as it is integrated into more direct means of human interaction, such as the telephone or television, which interface directly with our senses.

INTEGRATION

A good number of companies have tried to adapt to the need to be able to handle multiple ways of interacting. Still the business landscape is littered with the remains of businesses that implemented email, telephone or fax intake operations, only to discover they had no means to ensure that the information was integrated correctly once it was received by their businesses. Moreover, the embarrassment became even more acute when customers followed up with a phone call or a fax, asking what happened to their email.

To the customers' consternation, most of the time they never did find out, because phone calls went to one internal company department and faxes to another, and they never shared the information. In a memorable article published in the *Wall Street Journal*, fall 1996, entitled "Simplest email Queries Confound Companies," the author recounts the travails of blue-blood companies such as 3M, Coca-Cola, and MCI, which hadn't considered the need for information integration. The author concluded by observing: "For the time being, however, a more typical response to an email inquiry is this reply received on the Mercedes-Benz Web site: 'Thank you very much for your email.... It would be helpful if you could give us your post address."

This problem is the crux of the second part of the riddle of the three I's. We still don't understand information technology as a business tool and have little capability to act in integrative ways when it comes to the information received from differing input sources. This being the case, let's look at the requirement for information integration and understand the implications for us as we try to cope with the challenge of winning the information game. As the following figure suggests, we have two choices when it comes to dealing with information flowing into our companies from a variety of sources. We can pass it through into existing business stovepipe structures and hope. Or we can take time, look it over, and process it, making sure the information gets to the right place for action.

Solve the Riddle of Three I's

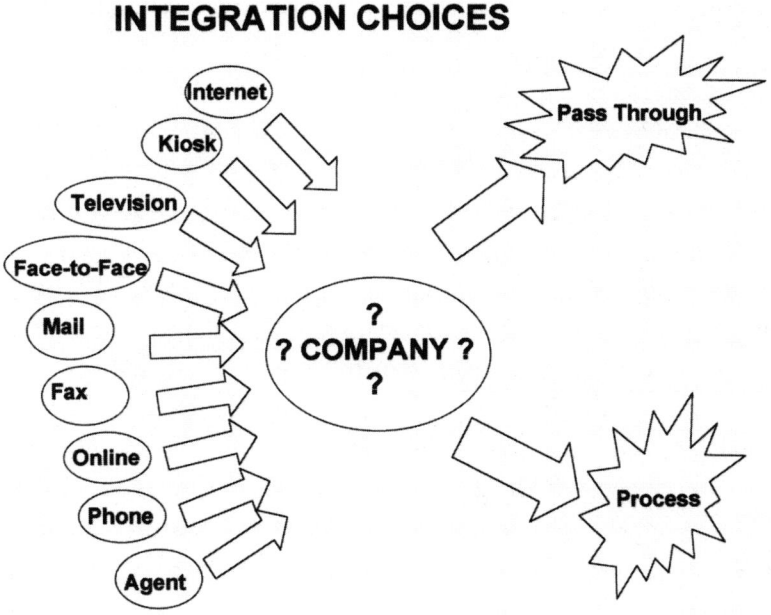

The road to trouble is to choose the stovepipe option. But at the same time in defense of those of us who do, the reason that information gets passed through into existing stovepipes is that when our companies go from interacting with customers to integration of the information that has been communicated, they assume integration. Or more probably they hope integration will take place somehow. Making assumptions can be a potentially fatal business activity any time, but it is even more so in today's business world.

Most of our internal stovepipe company processes are designed to reduce information to the form needed only by that stovepipe. Anything that does not fit the needed model or reports is discarded as irrelevant or unimportant. Once in a discussion with a respected senior researcher at a large company, I noted that the company discarded customer comments included on research surveys that had been returned.

When I asked why it did this, the answer was that the company didn't have the time or the resources to handle such data. And after all, it usually didn't have anything to do with the survey questions or research being accomplished. Such activity may be OK when doing focused research. When the aim is to drive information to promote solutions and results and create competitive advantage, it is absolutely the wrong answer.

If that's not enough, imagine this conversation, told to me by a business friend, and ask yourself: Does this happen in my company? It had to do with a misrouted phone customer who accidentally got shunted to the strategic planning department of his brokerage company. Customer: "The last time I called you, you sent me a prospectus for your money market fund. I was wondering if you could answer a few questions?" Staffer, like a deer caught in the lights of an onrushing car: "I'm sorry, but you have the strategic planning department." Customer: "Oh, that's great. I guess you could tell me where you think the fund will go, since you do all that planning stuff?" Staffer: "I'm sorry, sir, but we just do real plans here. Let me transfer you to the operator, and maybe they can direct you to someone else."

In contrast, taking the time to process and look the incoming feedback over, ensuring its proper packaging and dissemination offers us the potential for quite another outcome.

The faster things seem to come at us, the more there is a need for us and our people to take the time to sort through things, adding common sense and perspective. To do this, we don't ask that people be an expert at all the details. We ask only two things. First, we ask that they know where to send the information they process and package. Second, we ask that they package the information in ways that are useful to us, and that they then transmit the information in a timely fashion so we can respond better and faster. We know that companies who figure out how to make information work for them will be the winners in the 21st century business world. Here the answer is not to let the speed of the information age overwhelm us. Rather, it is to treat time strategically, and use it to our advantage by processing the input.

So the value proposition has actually been broadened, and that's the real answer to the question of why we need to take the route of making sure we process feedback rather than passing it through. In addition to affording us the opportunity to establish order, taking time to process the incoming feedback allows us to leverage technology and people in more effective and efficient ways that actually save time and resources in the long run. Moreover, it ensures accountability and judgment. And if done correctly, processing can promote flexibility and business learning.

With a commitment to processing the feedback before passing it on, the problem of interactivity is no longer a part of our riddle, it is an opportunity. Moreover, we have changed the issue of integration from a weakness to a strategic strength for our companies. And it should further be noted that while the discussion so far has focused on an externally focused operations, the same logic applies to tying internal company data sources together. We could just as easily create a processing capability that cleared, integrated and disseminated as internal operational data, financial data, employee feedback and product data.

Let's return for a moment to the idea of our human biological processes. We should remember that our brain is a processing center for external data received by the senses, as well as information received from the various internal systems, such as the circulatory system. Powerful synergy is achieved when they are linked and work in harmony rather than in opposition. Only one question remains: How do we organize our businesses to process feedback productively? That is the subject of the next two chapters.

INFORMATION

Before turning to the matter of processing feedback, there is still one piece of the riddle left for us to consider—the matter of information itself. The difficulty here is that if we are to cope with the challenges of the information age, we and our companies not only have to purposely set about focusing on feedback from our external and internal worlds. We must also take the time to know and define what information our businesses want and, more important, need before we start acting. Only then should we set about collecting, integrating and using information.

Unfortunately, this is the last activity most of us consider, if it is considered at all. Instead, we go about buying all sorts of technology, customer lists, and programs that bring in increasing amounts of data, gradually overwhelming and stifling operations. Then we rush out and buy more equipment to manage and store all of this data that hasn't been integrated, has no relevance, and no one ever looks at. The net result is that we create data-rich and information-poor companies that can't compete. As if to confirm this truth, *The Wall Street Journal* reported on its July 1, 1999 front page that Fuld & Co., a competitive intelligence firm in Cambridge, Massachusetts, interviewed seven corporate librarians and determined that companies fail to use as much as 70% of the online business data they buy.

If it were possible, some rational person should demand that we stop buying data, feedback, hardware and software with which to decorate our offices until we know what information we want. To solve the final part of the riddle, therefore, the first thing we need to do is to require that everyone, from the CEO to the lowest technician, specify what information they really think they need. This requirement should be based on the corporate vision and everyone's shared part in it. Some call this activity "Knowledge Management." I call it plain "Survival Smarts!"

A companywide inventory should be undertaken to determine the information needs. Once the resulting input is received, we then need to review it and create a user's information-needs map. For example, let's say that ten of our departments indicate they need one piece of information. Six departments report they need another. This is noted. Next, we group the information by focus, such as customer and competitor or new product information.

Solve the Riddle of Three I's

At the same time that our information needs are being determined, we should develop clear feedback collection guidelines to collect the feedback that facilitates our ability to drive movement toward achieving our shared business vision. I remember once visiting a large West Coast utility company that collects a lot of feedback on its competitors, and asking why it placed so much emphasis on information collection guidelines. The answer was short and sweet: "It keeps us focused, honest, and out of trouble with the law." I would add, when we think about it, that having collection guidelines also saves time, resources, and money.

When the inventory work is complete, then the types of information we need are clustered. Then we direct our people to collect the necessary feedback, according to the established collection guidelines, turning it into the information needed by processing it. Next, our user's preferred ways of receiving the information are determined so once the feedback is processed, the information can be distributed to those who indicate they need it in ways that are useful to them. Finally, we develop ways to share the lessons learned and actions taken with our entire business.

Information needs are not static, so we need to conduct periodic information needs inventories and modify our collection activities accordingly. But only after all these things are accomplished should we consider what hardware and software we need to do the job for our companies. Do we really need a turbo-charged information-age, road-hog machine, or will some economy model do the job? And what about all that software loaded on our machines that no one ever uses? Is it really necessary?

SOLVING THE RIDDLE

So then the answer to the riddle is INFORMATION, INTEGRATION, INTERACTIVITY not INTERACTIVITY, INTEGRATION, INFORMATION. Know first what information is needed. Then organize to ensure its systematic collection, processing, and dissemination. Finally, orient so as to leverage the power of information age interactivity and connect with our customers. In all this, remember to use the technology that does what *you* want it to

Winning the Information Game

do for *you*. You are in charge not the machine! We are now ready to take the next step to reinforce the conceptual picture we have drawn. Attention will now turn to a detailed look at the core, the engine that will drive our ability to win the information game—the information clearing house. It is the answer to what we need to do to process all that feedback and data.

CHAPTER IV

INFORMATION GAME SUMMARY

Step III: Solve the feedback riddle of acquiring, processing, and using information

Solving the riddle of the Three I's is the central external business challenge
- Interactivity provides the means to connect with our customers.
- Integration makes sure we process the information and get it to the right place in a timely fashion.
- Information is the processed feedback that the user needs to promote effective action.

The solution to the riddle of the Three I's is information, integration and interactivity, not interactivity, integration and then information. To succeed, we:
- Determine what information is needed first.
- Organize to ensure that the feedback collected gets processed, integrated, packaged, and disseminated to the right place in a timely fashion.
- Make sure we have the means to connect with our customers in the *ways* they prefer.
- Remember, use technology that does what *you* want it to do for *you*!

CHAPTER V

UNDERSTAND INFORMATION CLEARING HOUSES

*"Learn the fundamentals of the game
and stick to them. Band-Aid remedies never last."*
—Jack Nicklaus

Step four requires that we understand, deploy, and use information clearing houses if we are to process and handle all the data and feedback needed to win the information game. Because of the central importance of clearing houses to the effective processing of feedback, this chapter deals first with understanding what an information clearing house is. The next chapter will use practical examples to talk about deploying and using them.

OK, so what exactly is so critical about an information clearing house to leveraging and driving information? Historically, their value has been their ability to establish a sense of order. And we could certainly use a good dose of that today. The banking industry, for example, uses them as a means of clearing checks and balancing accounts. Security operations use them because they afford some sense of control over the access process.

Winning the Information Game

For most of the rest of us, however, we have tended to see them as mechanical, necessary, but not very innovative activities. All that has changed with the advent of the information age and its ability to swamp us with tons of stuff. We thought computers, electronic switches and the like would act as clearing houses and help with the overload. But you know what? All they have done is make matters worse. They have made the question—when is enough, enough?—a real issue for us and our companies. How many databases do we need? One? Ten? One hundred? And just for fun, who's in charge? Information clearing houses allow us to put more reason back into the process. More important, they put people back in charge of the machines—a key requirement if we are to process and drive things.

In fact, one of the more counterproductive spin-offs of the information age is the ability of data and feedback overload to freeze effective action. It is the ultimate irony. Today we are surrounded by fancy technology, and never have frustrations been higher. Everyone is talking about overload, from newscasters to icons like Bill Gates. Among the symptoms is the multitude of meetings and study groups that bedevil us and never seem to accomplish very much. Actually, they move us farther and farther away from the goal of leveraging and driving information.

Frankly, never has there been a greater need for a referee, a traffic cop, an information clearing house. I'm talking about a place where people have one aim in life: to make sense out of all the data, and speed it on its way as information to the right person in the right place at the right time.

When I asked a friend what he thought the value of information clearing houses is, he didn't hesitate. He said that they are the hammer needed to break today's information gridlock because they serve as a natural catalyst for action missing in our companies. I am a bit more modest about their potential. I like to think of information clearing houses as putting the business head back on the headless horseman, allowing us to process and integrate feedback effectively. That is, putting some backbone back into our business structure.

We shouldn't forget that by themselves, information clearing houses will never totally insulate us from business risk or doing dumb things. But they can certainly help us sort through all the "stuff" bombarding us. They can tell us more clearly what is going on, but they can not and should not tell us how to handle things.

Put another way, they can offer insights about how to get out of trouble, but they can't guarantee success. Information is always framed in the eye of the beholder.

A businessman was enjoying his favorite hobby—hot-air ballooning. He was flying when he discovered that he was lost. After reducing his height he spotted a man down below on the ground. The balloonist then lowered the balloon further and shouted: "Excuse me, sir, can you tell me where I am?"

The man, startled by the unexpected direction from which the voice came, looked up and replied, "Yes I can. You're in a hot-air balloon, hovering 30 feet above this field."

"You must work in Information Technology," replied the exasperated business balloonist. "Yes I do, but how did you know?" answered the man on the ground.

"Well," responded the balloonist, "Everything you have told me is technically correct, but it's of no use to anyone."

The man on the ground thought for a minute and said, "You must work in management." "You're right! But how did you know that?" replied the balloonist.

"Well!" responded the man, "You don't know where you are, or where you're going, but you expect me to be able to help. You're in the same position you were in before we met, but somehow it's all my fault."

CLEARING HOUSE RESPONSIBILITIES

As we seek to understand their responsibilities and what clearing houses can do for us, we need first to understand what they are not responsible for. Although clearing houses use databases extensively to store collected feedback for later trending and analysis, they are not data warehouses. Their real responsibility is to turn

Winning the Information Game

data into information through timely processing that includes integration and packaging, and then knowing where to send it.

Second, information clearing houses are not action agencies or fix-it shops. True, they collect feedback against established business needs and serve as early warning against developing business problems. Further, they may play the role of facilitator to bring people together to act on the feedback they have collected by initiating problem solving groups. But they are not accountable for producing the solutions and results—only facilitating them. Producing the desired result belongs to the group that receives the information and is operationally responsible for its use.

Those of us who receive information from our clearing houses can and must retain the right to do whatever we deem appropriate, even if those in the clearing house may wish otherwise. I used to remind people who worked with me in a clearing house setting that they had a right to have opinions about everything but the information they were transmitting for action. Those in the clearing house need to remain neutral and objective to the maximum extent practicable. It is up to others to place value and priority on the information.

The one exception to this rule is to vigorously protest when recipients try to tag the clearing house with the messenger label. Those in the clearing house must make the user understand that they are not the cause of the problem. Nor are they responsible for developing the solution. And the recipient has no right to try to "shoot the messenger!"

Information clearing houses are not the source of the data or information. Neither are they the cause of the problem. They are simply the messengers. Just because they may transmit some unpleasant piece of information that needs attention does not mean they have any sort of predisposition regarding that information. On too many occasions I have seen some especially critical piece of information passed to someone who needs it only to have the messenger roundly chastised for being the cause of the problem. "Oh, really?" should be the stock response. "Please shoot me on the spot if it will make you feel better and help you take action on the gift you are being given." You may make me go away but the problem will remain!"

A recently published book, entitled *Unleashing the Killer App, Digital Strategies for Market Dominance,* addresses the "shoot the messenger" syndrome in several ways. But most directly, the book's authors, Larry Downes and Chunka Mui, suggest that companies had better get a life and learn how to leverage Killer Apps because they are everywhere and will keep coming. What then are the responsibilities of the clearing house?

1. Leveraging information for competitive advantage. The first responsibility of an information clearing house is to leverage information for competitive advantage. Clearing houses are not nice-to-have operations. We put them in place to improve the bottom line by finding problems, identifying opportunities, and facilitating solutions and results, knowing that the faster we do it, the better. When the day is done, therefore, we have a simple metric to judge what value they have added and what others should be accountable for.

It is true that our companies have serious societal obligations in the late 20th century. But they are not here primarily to be social agencies. They are here to make an honest profit. In fact, by generating competitive advantage they are optimizing their ability to make a profit and also ultimately to discharge their social obligations. I have never seen a company at risk that was good at being an active community team player.

When we evaluate the efficiency and effectiveness of clearing houses, we should do so within the context of what they have done to promote solutions and results. While wanting to know their cost-benefit makes good rational business sense, we should also view clearing houses as an investment. Many times it will not be possible to totally quantify their value. This aspect of their value proposition became clear to me when I was provided a comment that read: "Thank you for just being there to listen—I know the company cares!"

2. Empowering employees. Having a group responsible for collecting, integrating, packaging, disseminating, and sharing information takes a huge load off of everyone's back, from the front-line employee to senior management. Everyone knows they are not alone. There is someone who will ensure that feedback provided gets to someone for attention and possible action. Just this realization is very empowering, and it can quickly improve results. It tells everyone that they don't have to carry the load alone. They are part of a team, and their input is valued.

In the time I have been involved with helping people learn to leverage and drive information, I have been encouraged by how much companies have begun to listen to their employees. In winning companies, without exception, management has found that they are to be trusted as valued partners. They are wonderful sources of information about operational shortfalls, competitor initiatives, and what is going on in the heads of our customers. When management listens and responds, everyone shares and empowered business behavior increases.

I experienced a very real example of this information-driven empowerment when touring an automobile assembly line a few years ago. Our guide pointed to a button near the assembly line and then observed that it was responsible for the biggest improvement in productivity and safety the company had experienced in years. When pushed by any of the workers, it immediately shut down the assembly line.

So how did it increase productivity? For years employees had watched cars come by with defects. They had no way of letting anyone else know. One time, when management asked for ways to improve productivity, the employees voiced the idea of giving everyone the power to stop the assembly line when they saw something wrong. At first, stoppages were pretty regular. Gradually they decreased. At the end of the assembly line fewer and fewer cars were failing the exhaustive quality check. By the end of the first year, the plant won an award for improved safety and productivity, and it hasn't looked back since.

There is one catch to all of this: We must always remember that our operational window for making good use of information is very short and is getting shorter all the time in the information age.

Understand Information Clearing Houses

It's a known fact that the person who gets the information first is the one who stands to benefit the most. This thought should be a fundamental operating axiom of the information age. And it should put all business researchers on notice. The old line research model is under attack because the results it provides come so long after they are needed that it often generates more business frustration rather than less. Based on a lot of practical business and operational experience, I visualize the information value–time continuum as depicted below. For business operators it can be reduced to a single thought regarding information: the faster we get it, the better—win, lose, or draw!

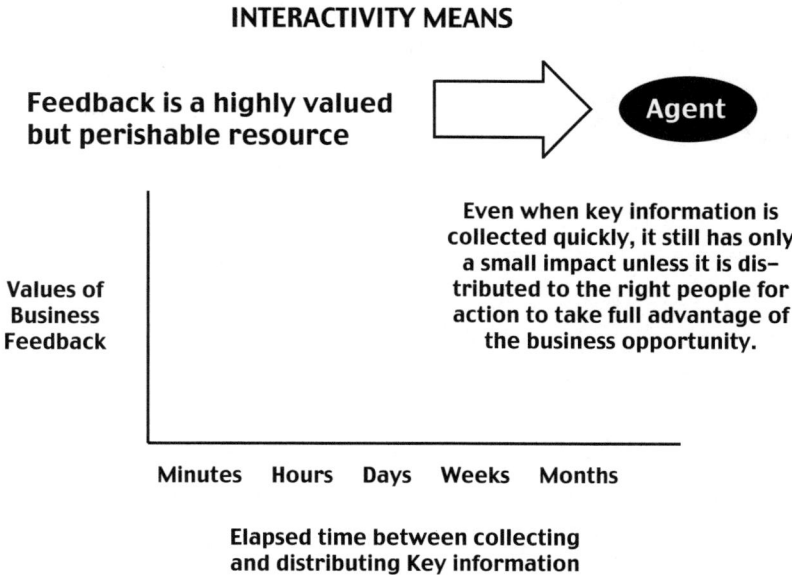

3. Promote customer relations. In the case of car production, if the product has fewer flaws then, obviously there is the potential to improve customer relations as well as profits. But there is another even more important outcome from this clearing house responsibility. The fact that the information gets to someone for action quicker and in a better packaged fashion means that it can be followed up on faster.

Just the act of showing interest in what a customer or an employee has to say can generate positive returns for our companies far out of proportion to the work involved. A business colleague reported to me how timely responses to customer input can be very effective. Her company's letter handling and clearing unit passed on a comment from a customer that suggested a change to the company's primary product to make it better. On a whim she decided to follow up on the comment and called the customer. He was so flattered by the interest, she reported, that even today she continues to hear from the customer, and he always professes his undying loyalty to the company and its products, all because of the attention given to his feedback.

4. Foster communications. This clearing house responsibility may seem misplaced. What does a clearing house have to do with fostering communications? It is a sad fact, in all too many of our companies today, that communications across departmental and subsidiary boundaries are at best limited. In a lot of cases they are nonexistent. By having a clearing house whose focus is disseminating and sharing information, we rapidly realize that there is no such thing as marketing information or planning information. Rather, in its most effective form, information has value to almost everyone inside the business. It's the other businessman or woman, our competitors, outside our companies that we want to watch. And our clearing houses are ideal vehicles to do this too.

When the information clearing house distributes information for action, those of us who must respond quickly realize that we can't go it alone. It really takes a team effort to win. Marketers must talk to planners, and operators must talk to sales people. There is nothing that warms the heart of an old messenger more than to see this information clearing house effect in action!

Sometimes clearing houses are so good they seem to give us the answers before we think of the questions. But be warned. As

Understand Information Clearing Houses

much as we would like, clearing houses can't predict the future. If they tried, I'm afraid they would end up like the fortune teller in the following vignette. A business person, sick and tired of getting blindsided by his competitors, wanted better information and a better view of the future, so he decided to visit a psychic as a last resort. But when he knocked on the psychic's door and the psychic called out, "Who's there?" the business person promptly left!

5. Create a positive business climate. How in the world is an information clearing house to be responsible for creating a positive business climate when one of its tasks is to identify problems? If we are more worried about who's to blame for the problem rather than creating a positive business climate, it might be a problem. My view of clearing houses is that because they disseminate the information for action, they also have the right to influence how people get rewarded for responding.

What's wrong with celebrating the fact that someone has fixed a problem rather than dwelling on the negative aspect of the problem itself? After all, maybe the problems won't come back at all if we put all our energy into recognizing better and better fixing behaviors. And it's a heck of a lot more fun to catch people doing good things. Contrast this with the finger pointing and witch hunts that occur all too often when a problem surfaces. First, this is not productive behavior. Second, it costs a lot of money and resources. Finally, it does nothing to promote the bottom line and only causes people to cover up problems.

CLEARING HOUSE FUNCTIONS

The functions of an information clearing house are straightforward. It's the manner in which the functions are accomplished that gets a little complex. First, you collect. Second, you process and integrate what has been collected. Third, you disseminate what has been integrated to those of us who need it. Finally, you ensure that the solutions and results generated from the disseminated information are shared with the rest of the business. However, all of these activities are accomplished continuously and simultaneously by a number of units in the clearing house for

Winning the Information Game

all levels of the company. Here's where the process can get a bit complex. Let's address the functions in more detail.

1. Collect. If the collection effort is to be useful, it is obvious that the first thing we need to do is decide what it is we want to collect. Back to the idea of our five senses. Our eyes are responsible for one type of feedback input and our ears another—visual and auditory, for example. At this point, the specific kinds of information required within a category and the methods used to collect the data are not important. That comes later as we begin to refine the collection structure, get feedback from our users, and improve our own clearing house operations.

In the case of our businesses, comparable data types to sensory inputs of interest can include employee, customer, and competitor feedback. Once we decide if we will collect one or all types, then we focus on the means and methods. Basically there are two methods—active and passive. Active collection measures are those we initiate, such as customer satisfaction surveys, focus groups and the like. We control and initiate them, and they seek to extract data for integration and dissemination. Market research, for example, primarily uses active means of data collection. Passive measures are those we set up that are not under our control but provide the opportunity for input if the initiator so chooses. Employee suggestion boxes are one example. Another is creating ways to collect freely provided customer comments.

A key point to remember, however, is that agreement on what feedback will be collected or what questions will be asked, whether active or passive, needs to be obtained prior to starting any collection activity. Too often, I have seen feedback collected, only to have it suppressed. Nothing will destroy the credibility and trust in a clearing house faster than to have this happen. It is better not to ask the question at all than to ask it and suppress the answer.

Finally, we organize into units to collect the input. If we decide to organize on the basis of the type of feedback we seek, such as customer and employee feedback, then we would probably use some combination of active and passive methods to do so. However, if we decide that we would rather organize by a method such as having a unit that uses active surveys to collect the data, then we would have to make sure we didn't omit any data types—employees, customers, or competitors.

Either way, what is collected is fed to a data warehouse where it can be accessed, processed and integrated or sent immediately on to an area for action and use. Ultimately, the data is stored in the warehouse for subsequent analysis and tracking. Throughout the process, however, the unit that collects the data retains responsibility for its integration, dissemination, and tracking to ensure that the information gets to where it needs to go and solutions and results are shared.

In summary, for collection purposes, clearing house units can be organized around specific types of input or methods of collection—it makes no difference. For example, you might create a unit that collects all incoming customer feedback from a single access channel. Access channels refer to the various ways a customer can interact with a business, such as over the phone or with a computer, or even face-to-face. Another unit might collect data on competitors, and yet another unit might collect employee inputs. The mixing and matching of units inside such an operation can be virtually unlimited. The point is, once clearing house units have been given responsibility to collect something, they retain it throughout the entire collection, processing and integration, and dissemination and sharing parts of the process.

2. Process and Integrate. Based on established information priorities that flow from our departments, each information clearing house unit processes and integrates what it has collected. The goal is packaging the feedback and getting it to the right area just as fast as possible to promote fixing things and achieving solutions and results. Once this is done then people in the unit count and analyze what they have collected, warehousing it in common access databases so it can be used further for trending and systemic, long-range analysis.

Unlike more formal research means, the analysis done by the unit is focused on identifying opportunities and problems that need action rather than statistical rigor. The area receiving the integrated information is responsible for determining its relevance. Trends rather than statistical significance are the focus. Getting the word out rather than waiting until you are absolutely certain what is going on is the aim. There is time for counting and statistical rigor later.

In fact, in more sophisticated clearing houses, there may also be a strategic integration unit charged with responsibility for taking all the data stored in the various unit clearing house data warehouses and doing the more sophisticated analysis and trending. This unit may also do independent new research to verify what the other clearing house units are uncovering, if needed. When this function is performed, however, the integration unit like the other clearing house units, bears responsibility for disseminating and sharing the solutions and results generated from its effort.

3. Disseminate. The responsibility for getting the integrated information to business users clearly resides with our information clearing house. It points out the reality that we are dealing with a circular process that must be managed from start to finish by each of the units in the clearing house for its particular type of information. If there is an integration unit, then it is responsible for integrating all the looped clearing house unit processes and managing the resulting more global circular process. If we don't do this, sustaining the process is virtually impossible. All parts of the clearing house simultaneously and continually collect, integrate, disseminate, and share solutions and results. So once the whole process is running and managed, it becomes self-supporting and self-correcting.

While the information is different, the various clearing house units many times use the same communications channels to disseminate their information. What is different is that the information goes to different places and is usually handled by different people. However, our people who receive a particular kind of information work with their clearing house unit on a continuing basis, forming a virtual action network. They work the information received, generating the solutions and results. The continuing relationship also keeps them abreast of trends and allows them to keep the clearing house unit informed when information needs change.

Understand Information Clearing Houses

4. Share. There are lots of great things going on all over our companies all the time. Think of the competitive power we could generate if we could just share what we did to fix a problem, change a customer misperception, remove the barriers that keep our employees from giving their all, or just complimenting people for a job well done! This is probably the most important job of the information clearing house. I call the activity "closing feedback loops." Sharing is the springboard to business learning, and it can prevent us from making the same mistake again, and again, and again. It is the essence of real—and I repeat real—knowledge management.

Within our departments that receive information for action from clearing house units, agents who form virtual teams across the company work the packaged information. To ensure that the feedback loop is closed, these agents now have the obligation and must be required to update the common data warehouses, where the information is stored. When they do this, they indicate what they did with the information to fix things so everything can be shared. In effect, we now have a linking engine, an information clearing house that links everything together. The people in the clearing house then communicate the lessons throughout the business so we all win.

Interestingly, one of the more effective examples of this sort of activity is a military one. If you look on the Web, you will come across the CALL Web site—Center for Army Lessons Learned. Its primary job is to collect good ideas and lessons learned from people and units all over the U.S. Army. Then they make sure they are available and are shared with everyone. CALL has been around for a while, and there are those who credit CALL with being one of the key contributors to the Army's success in Desert Storm, where we took on Iraq and won a stunning free-world coalition victory.

As I raised my arm in triumph at making the foregoing comment to an audience of my peers, a hand shot up. "OK, what happens if I share something and the other managers don't share anything in return." I was startled, but the comment raised an interesting point. We have been conditioned to go it alone for so long that to reach out and take a chance in disclosing our best practices inside the company seems like suicide. How strange!

We'll go to great lengths to benchmark other companies and guard our information from outsiders. Now we've got to wake up and realize that whether we like one another or not, inside the company are the only real business friends we have. If we don't start sharing our information, we will all lose.

HOW TO START AN INFORMATION CLEARING HOUSE

The figure below depicts the steps in starting a clearing house. All the steps are designed to support a circular information process that, if focused on the user, ties management to dissemination in a continuous manner.

1. Identify the information needs of the user. Very clearly the first step is to identify the information needs of the user. Any number of approaches can be used, but for most companies undertaking a complete information needs assessment is probably most useful because it can also become a means to discard or consolidate unwanted information gathering.

2. Create a data warehouse. Once we have identified the information we need to collect, we need to create a data warehouse. It is here that the data collected will be stored. Most often we will want the warehouse to be separate, yet have relational characteristics so we can take advantage of other databases that exist in our companies. Either way, the importance of having a good data warehouse cannot be overstated, because it becomes the source of our ability to do more sophisticated operations, such as trending and forecasting.

3. Establish collection and reporting methods. We must have the procedures in place to know what to do with what we collect. Who should get the information? Where will we store it in the data warehouse? How do we update and purge our databases? The list goes on and on, but this step ensures that we can go to effective packaging so we can deliver to users what they need, when they need it.

Understand Information Clearing Houses

4. Make the information actionable and useful. To do this we have to keep a finger on the needs pulse of our users. Just because we have collected something doesn't mean it is useful or actionable. In our fast-moving business worlds, value added is synonymous with information that provides a competitive advantage or gets a leg up on the other person. This kind of information must be provided first every time, all the time. It requires that the people who manage the information clearing house stay in constant touch with their users, and that they be willing and able to change their systems, collection, and storage methods at a moment's notice. When all parts of the process work in harmony, we have truly created a business analog to the biological processes that make humans so adaptable.

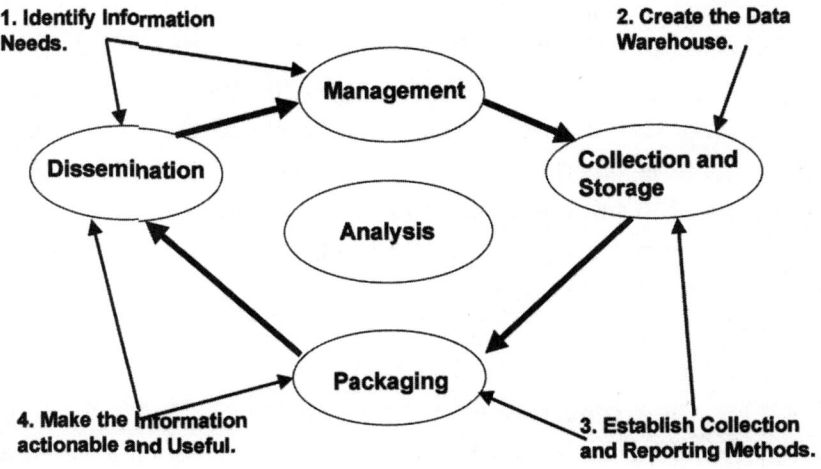

STEPS IN STARTING AN INFORMATION CLEARING HOUSE

OPERATING A CLEARING HOUSE

Operating a clearing house is a four-step process that summarizes everything to this point in this chapter.

1. Stop thinking linearly and start thinking in terms of feedback loops. Throw out the idea that anything in the information age needs to be done in a sequential fashion. We can certainly always count, analyze and then decide to fix something. But does it make sense to use this strategy when we have the means to be fixing, counting, and analyzing things continuously and simultaneously? What if we are thinking linearly and our competitors are thinking in looped fashion? I think the answers are obvious.

2. Make technology work for you and your business. All the activities involved in organizing the clearing house have technological components. A few years back we couldn't even begin to envision or understand the capability of electronic integration that exists today. From the telephone to the television to the computer, information can and does move in an increasingly seamless fashion.

Our job in operating the clearing house is to ensure that we make it do what we want. I had a discussion with a friend one time about all the inefficient wiring that sticks out and around and over our computers. He was worried about how to shorten and tie all the wires together to improve efficiency. I told him that unless he was a neatness freak, such efforts were a waste of time. With things that move at the speed of light, distance is no longer critical unless you are going to run the wires around the moon a couple of times. Far more important is to make sure the wires go to the right place and are connected to the right data warehouse. Then you make sure that you have the right programs and machines on line. Finally, if you have time, you bundle the wires neatly.

3. Develop supporting teams. Specifically, I am talking about the real people teams that inhabit our clearing houses and companies. They need the same old leadership and development they always have. Further, they need to feel appreciated and wanted, although the life of a messenger can be trying at times. But I am also talking about another team—our virtual teams.

Understand Information Clearing Houses

When you look at what is said about virtual teams today, you are almost left with the sense that they just happen—that they are magic! Nothing is further from the truth. They need to be developed and led. Where distance is concerned, trust is more important, not less important. While we may not interact face-to-face with virtual teams, they are still composed of people. The more we make them real, the better will be the operation of the clearing house and our companies as a whole.

4. Just start doing it. Don't wait to put together the perfect clearing house operation. And for goodness' sake don't wait for the perfect technology. It just doesn't exist. I think waiting for perfection or the perfect solution is one of the biggest cop-outs of the information age. Never have we had more opportunities to make it happen. So what if we only get a ten percent improvement? Later on, as long as we seek to make that a twenty percent improvement, then thirty percent and so forth, we will always be ahead of the power curve. The real secret of the clearing house is that it allows us to do things better, faster, and then do the same thing, very powerfully, again and again and again and again. Now let's turn to the second part of this step to market domination and address the matters of deploying and using clearing houses to win the information game.

CHAPTER V

INFORMATION GAME SUMMARY

Step IV: Understand, deploy, and use information clearing houses

The information clearing house is the natural catalyst for action missing in our companies today. Information clearing houses are not
- Data warehouses.
- Action agencies or fix it shops.
- The cause of the problem.

Clearing houses are responsible for
- Leveraging information for competitive advantage.
- Empowering employees.
- Promoting customer relations.
- Fostering communications.
- Creating a positive business climate.

The information clearing house functions are
- To collect.
- To process and integrate.
- To disseminate.
- To share.

CHAPTER VI

DEPLOY AND USE CLEARING HOUSES

"The future belongs to those who believe in the beauty of their dreams."
—*Eleanor Roosevelt*

Where is the evidence that what we have been talking about so far is anything more than interesting theory? What are the indicators of successful practice? Although not always conclusive, for starters, we need go no further than the popular business press. One can infer from recent reports on the profitability and success of the major airlines in blue-plate publications, such as *Fortune* magazine, that market leaders like Southwest Airlines are also the ones that are positioning themselves and their employees to drive information and leverage the growing capabilities of the information age.

THE EVIDENCE

From handling reservations, to the check-in counter, to the boarding gate, to general customer service, and finally to having fun during the flight, businesses like Southwest Airlines have deployed aspects of clearing house operations to drive information and make it work for them. Moreover, the managers and leaders tasked with making things happen are empowered to facilitate and integrate things to reach their shared corporate vision. As Southwest customers keep flocking back, one has to conclude that they must believe that they are dealing with a first-class company that knows how to make information do what it wants it to do!

Another example of a company that has deployed aspects of clearing house operations and that has worked hard to leverage information and drive things is AT&T Universal Card, now Universal Card Services, in Jacksonville, Florida. To visitors who observe its use of immediate feedback, it is evident that Universal Card is integrating and using information from multiple sources to improve responsiveness to customer needs. Organizationally, Universal Card has used information to drive many functions, such as pay and benefits and the manning and training of customer-contact employees. The result–facilitators, called *associates* by Universal Card, service customers rather than take orders. It is a responsive, adaptable, and virtually invisible technology support system, and the profits are good!

Pillsbury has advanced even further and has been leveraging the power of information from its employees to improve operations and its competitive position since 1993. Employees can telephone a third-party clearing agent anonymously, where the information is transcribed, integrated, and passed on for action. It is reported that every transcript reaches the hands of the company's CEO, and the results have been gratifying. The company uses a focused clearing house model to achieve its results. Moreover, its understands the importance of treating information as a circular feedback loop process in the manner described in the previous chapter. Thomas Petzinger, a business writer, concluded regarding the Pillsbury example, "The best way to get people to speak up is to prove you're listening—and the best way to prove you're listening is to act on what people say."

Looking farther across the business landscape, lots of other companies work with employee feedback, collect information on their competitors, and listen to their customers. Ford Motor Company has a complaint center. General Electric has a sophisticated help center. However, most often, information collection focuses on only one or two major types of information, for example, employee feedback or customer complaints. While this is progress, it certainly doesn't begin to maximize the potential of the information available. We are left to wonder why the will to systematically engage in such activities is so slow in developing.

A 1995 article by the Futures Group, a Glastonbury, Connecticut, research firm, called "Ostriches and Eagles," framed the business issue clearly. The Futures Group found that while companies professed an intense understanding of the need for information about competitors, American business was moving slowly and unevenly to develop capabilities to do so. The group lamented, "Barely half . . . of the respondents had an organized system that provides competitive, technological or business intelligence."

THE GAP AND THE INNOVATORS

I speak to a lot of people about feedback and information issues. During discussions, I am constantly encouraged by the interest in the subject. At the same time, I am struck with the general sense of confusion about how to go about doing what needs to be done. But most significantly, I am stunned by the tone of sad resignation I hear: "That could never work in my company!"

Fortunately, there are a number of innovators who have had the courage to cross the gap to use and deploy information clearing houses for their good and the good of their customers and partners. The remaining parts of this chapter touch on three companies that can offer us insight and inspiration. First, there is USAA, a financial services company that has pioneered the internal use of clearing houses for the benefit of its operations and its customers. In recognition of its efforts, USAA's Feedback Operation was awarded Arthur Andersen's WorldWide Customer Satisfaction Best Practices Award for 1997 and had its operations described in the book *Best Practices: Building Your Business with Customer-Focused Solutions* by Andersen Associates Hiebeler, Kelly, and Kettelman.

Second, a new company, Direct1, has developed an automated external clearing house process and system that is helping its business customers and partners achieve new competitive advantage. Finally, there is the software and consulting giant, Computer Sciences Corporation (CSC), which is again demonstrating its leadership as an innovator. CSC has already incorporated a real time feedback system into its network outsourcing operations so that it can quickly identify problem areas and demonstrate the ability to meet guaranteed service levels.

To protect the privacy of the companies used as examples, the comments which follow and detail their feedback processes have been limited to that which is available in the public domain and information that supports the larger theme of this book. If you would like more detail, I invite you to read some of the more comprehensive accounts listed in the references and readings section of this book.

Let us now turn to a discussion of inside and outside information clearing houses and CSC's business application of the capability. We will conclude our discussion with a review of the lessons we can learn from these examples in our quest to become competent information drivers.

THE INSIDE EXAMPLE: USAA

Let's turn first to the example of deploying and using clearing houses to manage feedback at USAA. It can provide insights as we work to develop and manage organizational processes dedicated totally to collecting, facilitating, integrating and helping our businesses use feedback to drive information.

The publicly stated departmental task of USAA's feedback clearing house, as noted in the *Bests' Review* article "Companies can Benefit from Feedback Engineering," flows from the company's core vision of service to its members (customers). It is to bring the power of feedback to new levels by facilitating solutions and results that promote better customer service and remove business barriers.

USAA has always believed in being responsive to its members. Its culture promotes an enduring employee desire to care for them. Customers actually own the company. Moreover, it is one of the pioneers in the leveraging of technology to support business practices. Frustration about seeing the same service problems over and over again led USAA to form what today is a fully functional, internal information clearing house.

THE INTERNAL CLEARING HOUSE

Again, as noted in *Bests Review*, that wasn't the case in late 1994, although some information collection activities had been ongoing for a couple of years. Then the word went out to pull all customer and employee feedback activities together in one location. The challenges were significant. There were a number of separate systems, little task differentiation within the department, a lack of necessary skills, and a strong sense of allegiance to old stovepipe ways of doing things. On the positive side, however, was a firm belief at the company's most senior levels in the importance of getting better at driving information to promote solutions and results.

The interest and support of the senior leadership proved critical. The shared vision and support of the CEO and the other company seniors have been and will always be important to moving a business forward. It is absolutely vital in such areas as feedback collection, analysis, and management, where egos and sensitivities can dominate. It was this kind of vision at USAA that helped its management recognize the need to use information better. Paul Ringenbach noted in his book *USAA, A Tradition of Service, 1922-1997*, that CEO, General Herres, valued real-time data and in 1994 had all these information-collecting functions automated and gathered into one unit.

Faced with the task of getting things organized immediately to start adding value, the new departmental staff was forced to think creatively and do it quickly. Because the goal was to promote solutions and results, the staff had to change the order of the old problem/solution

Winning the Information Game

model from count, analyze, and then recommend/fix to fixing things first. They had a number of resources they could leverage.

First, electronic systems existed that were embedded in the operational structure. They facilitated and allowed connection of any feedback gathered directly with someone who could act on it. Second, distinct types of feedback were now being funneled into one department—surveys, direct and indirect customer feedback, and employee feedback. This allowed creation of a group of action teams organized by feedback type and supported by electronic links to others across the enterprise who could act on the feedback and then report back what they did.

The solution wasn't perfect, but the clearing house efforts did adhere to the concepts of good information collection and use—organize and orient to collect; collect; promote action and collect again. When I am asked by companies if they need sophisticated systems to become better at leveraging and driving information, the answer I always give is no! Companies just need to be willing to begin acting in ways that make information responsive to them.

USAA's evolving clearing house team had to accept that there would be inefficiencies in what they were doing. As a startup operation they reported that they were lucky to be 30% efficient. And, in a world that spends years trying to get a 100% solution before implementation, this seemed like suicide. However, USAA felt that the improved effectiveness in promoting solutions and results was worth it. They were proven right.

As the clearing house continued to develop, the leadership realized that having internal units that focused on one type of information process was good, but it didn't foster wider information integration. They had merely recreated miniature stovepipes responsive to a single manager. It maximized focused solutions and results, but did not get at the larger systemic and operational issues that were also identified. As a result, they created a departmental integration team.

The integration unit's job was to constantly scan all types of feedback being handled, drawing out the larger trends, issues, and solutions and sharing them with the entire company. In 1994 when the feedback integration process started, their task was quite manageable. At the end of 1997, it was reported that the department was integrating, distributing for action, counting, and analyzing over 25,000 pieces of feedback monthly. The job became more difficult because the supporting data warehouses from the inherited feedback systems were not tied together. Therefore, accomplishing feedback integration remained an extremely complicated manual process. Some manual integration will always remain when it comes to integrating information effectively. Fortunately, technology offers USAA and all of us solutions for the future.

At this point, USAA now had a closed loop information processing system and had linked it all together. Further, the focus was on fixing things and promoting solutions and results. To say users were happy with the new sources of information cascading down on them would be a gross misstatement.

Quite the contrary, as the *Journal of Retail Banking Services* article "ECHO System Helps USAA Listen – and Respond – to Customer Feedback" noted, only the support of the CEO and other seniors kept things going on days when the hunt for the messenger was on in earnest. The resistance was significant as users negatively saw everything as more work. So they shifted the emphasis to showing users how to win with feedback.

Over the next year it was reported that some 250 training sessions were conducted with internal company users in which everyone in the department worked on helping them improve their analysis and problem solving skills. The flaw had been to assume that managers could do their own analysis and interpretation without help. The absolute volume of undifferentiated industrial-age stuff coming down on them for so long had blinded them to the need to be their own analysts.

USAA is by no means alone with this problem. This skills gap is a very serious problem in most late twentieth-century businesses. In addition, the industrial-age model of having experts spoon-feed the user added to the problem because it obviates any need in many business professionals' minds to do their own analysis.

Such problems will remain with us awhile longer. Like it or not, USAA's feedback clearing house probably will continue to perform a necessary training function that complicates its ability to perform its primary clearing house functions. Again, the speed of information age actions and changes is blurring training and development responsibility, making it necessary for everyone to get involved in the business of company training.

This is the same reason it is so important that users be able to do their own analysis. In operations, the speed of information flow also renders other approaches far too slow and cumbersome. Further, we can't have a fully functioning and complete circular information process unless all players have the needed skills. Partly because of skill problems, one of the reported challenges at USAA to this day is to get users to report to the clearing house what they did with the feedback so they can share their wins with the rest of the company—closing feedback loops.

To share some of the flavor of the scope of USAA's clearing house operations, public sources reported that as of the end of 1997, they were annually fielding almost 400,000 customer surveys. In addition, they were collecting over 100,000 pieces of customer feedback a year through other means. Finally, on an annual basis they were handling over 8,000 items of employee feedback through an input network of 7,000 employees and a 300-employee companywide output action network of virtual and real teams.

EVERY CONTACT HAS OPPORTUNITY (ECHO™)

The core of USAA's internal operation, regardless of the type of feedback, is an electronic, system-supported, nerve network called ECHO™. More than 6,000 customer contact employees are tied into ECHO™ through USAA's core operational system, which also supports the delivery of service to its customers.

This distinction is critical. By embedding the feedback system in its operational systems USAA made sure that the resulting feedback couldn't be ignored. Moreover, since the system is engineered to include all components needed to ensure service problem solutions, it can also be enhanced to promote solutions to feedback

Deploying and Using Clearing Houses

issues. The mistake a lot of companies make is to make the information collection and dissemination system separate or parallel to their operational systems. The result is stonewalling and isolation of the information from those who need to see and handle the feedback. In short, separating information collection and dissemination systems from operational systems makes it easier for our existing business functions to ignore reality.

The reported rules for ECHO's™ use at USAA are simple: inputs are voluntary and must be beyond USAA's customer contact employees' power to fix. Further, inputs must have something to do with company operations. Beyond that, the sky is the limit. Even though the feedback many times needs to be verified because it is passive, unstructured input and does not adhere to statistical conventions, it proves to be a marvelous source of early warning.

On a weekly basis, it is reported, USAA employees enter close to 2,000 pieces of feedback into ECHO™. The feedback is then instantly sent to action agents across USAA for action. Action agents can assign the feedback to someone for fixing, verification, or monitoring. In any event, those in the clearing house, as well as anyone else who wants to, can track what is happening, share seen trends with senior management and the rest of the business, and make sure the lessons learned get shared. All this without interfering in the process or getting in the way.

What is actually happening, according to reports, is that the feedback is being put into one big data warehouse that everyone is hooked into. Visualize a great big glass ball with lots of wires going into it. Keeping with the principle of information visibility, people can look in at everyone else's feedback and even see what they are doing with it if they want. In fact, users are encouraged to view and learn from others.

If they are working on a special issue, other departments can even query the data warehouse to see how widespread the issue is without regard for where the feedback went for action—study trends on credit card feedback, for example. The only thing that can't be done is something that changes the feedback itself or changes its status. The action agent in the department or area who

Winning the Information Game

owns the feedback can only do that. So, in making and keeping the feedback visible, USAA increases the likelihood that something will be done with it. I used to tell people that it puts the normative power of "shame" back in vogue as a motivator. "Shame on you for not working your feedback, because I can still see it!!" How different from the industrial-age practice of hiding information.

For those providing customer feedback, the system is quick and simple. It takes customer contact employees less than 30 seconds to use the system. To initiate things they click on an embedded ECHO™ icon and a screen appears which prompts the user to select the feedback category desired. In USAA's case, categories such as service and claims handling are important.

Once a category is selected, another screen appears which provides the opportunity for employees to provide the necessary details, do a basic "root cause" analysis, and add any short comments desired. When the entry is complete, they click "send," and the feedback goes into the "glass ball," and action agents are alerted that they have feedback for processing, action, or resolution. The employee sending the feedback goes back to his customer and completes documenting the transaction.

One interesting fact about the creation of ECHO™, which anyone contemplating creating such an internal system should remember is that all the screens, categories, and "root cause" listings were created on the basis of input from the customer contact employees. They, in turn, tried to be as faithful as possible to the problems and issues raised by customers. Only then did the requirements get transmitted to the systems experts. For their part, the systems people were thrilled. They were actually responding to a concrete and identified business information need.

We should not be misled. ECHO™ is not a fixed or unchangeable system. Employees are constantly inputting changes and upgrades. For example, there is now an employee feedback component that focuses on employee needs and barriers to service. But it is not open-ended. The same feedback loop concept used with all other USAA processes exists, and there is an action network established where there is confidence that action will be taken.

When ECHO™ was designed, capabilities to change information screens, add types of feedback, and add action agents were all engineered into the system. Truly, ECHO™ at USAA is a living system that can be changed to meet USAA's information needs as they change. The following figure depicts generally how the process is reported to work

As this book went to press, the fully electronic ECHO™ system was in its fifth year, and I'm sure USAA continues to learn new

THE ECHO™ SYSTEM AT WORK!

```
Customer Employee Competitor Feedback  →  Clearing House Receives Information
                    ↓
              CIRCULAR SYSTEM
                    ↓
Results Shared and New Feedback Generated  ←  Feedback Captured, Packaged, and Sent Out For Action
                    ↑
              Area Sends Results to Clearing House
```

things every day. Reportedly, one of the more valuable features that has come of age is the ability of staff and management to ask customer contact employees hooked into ECHO™ to be on the lookout for and report special kinds of information for them—sort of a "by request" customer dialogue capability.

The advisories requesting specific input from customer contact employees are called HOT TOPICS. In one instance, some underwriting changes were made in a part of USAA's auto insurance policy. Employees were asked through a HOT TOPIC to report when they heard what the customers thought about the changes. Well, USAA discovered it had missed the point very quickly, but because of HOT TOPIC feedback, USAA was able to fix things in record time, reinforcing the power of proactive use of information-age technology embedded in ECHO™ to act as an early warning sentinel.

THE OUTSIDE EXAMPLE: DIRECT1

Increasingly, companies are reaching out beyond the walls of their businesses to form information alliances that produce more efficient and profitable results. A number of companies have moved into this world which specialize in such activities as data mining, customer relationship management, knowledge management, and consulting to improve information flow and use. Some are enjoying more success than others, as *The Wall Street Journal* noted in a headline on its July 1, 1999, front page which read, "EXPENSIVE UNUSED DATA are clogging up budgets and decision-making."

THE EXTERNAL CLEARING HOUSE

Direct1 is a unique example of an external clearing house that offers clearing house-based feedback processing and delivery similar to what USAA has done. But it does so as an extension of the company it supports rather than as an insider. In so doing, it offers robust new capabilities to companies that are reaching out for ways to get control of their destinies and drive information. Some of the characteristics of Direct1's operations that dovetail with the characteristics of clearing houses discussed in the last chapter include these:
- They offer help without falling into the consultant trap, yet they provide continuous advice and support.
- They can collect feedback in virtually any form—phone, internet, paper.
- They provide the most advanced technology without requiring businesses to purchase truckloads of new hardware.
- Their clearing house offerings include sophisticated feedback packaging and analysis.

Deploying and Using Clearing Houses

- They customize and display outputs in forms that are meaningful and useful to operators, enhancing the ability to take immediate action.
- They have automated their operations to the point that they can deliver information virtually instantaneously to users after it is collected, and change the feedback collection and output on the fly to adapt to changing user information needs.

Direct1's stated business aim is to give managers and leaders across user companies operational tools that provide continuous real-time insights into what customers, competitors and employees are thinking right now. In a sense, what they offer is a business equivalent of an EKG machine, an MRI machine, or a host of other medical clearing house diagnostic tools that provide doctors with the capability to monitor their patients—real time. Like the medical equipment providers, Direct1 assumes users have the expertise and desire to interpret and respond to what they see.

Direct1's proprietary analysis and information-packaging capabilities add approximately the equivalent of a 100-person research and support company to user company staffs at minimal cost. What they have done is take the manual processing and analysis function mentioned in the USAA example and automate it using some very advanced, proprietary programming. The analysis engine that takes the place of all the people is called AutoQuest™. But what makes the value proposition so attractive is that the feedback system becomes a virtual extension of a company's own Intranet or communications network, and it's very easy and cost-effective to install, customize, and operate.

Just as with the USAA example, Direct1 adds value and provides a unique business capability in three ways. First, it provides real time information focused on promoting solutions and results for managers, partner businesses, and customers. In effect, it fills a gap in that it provides operational rather than research information in a timely fashion to operators. Second, it deploys a total electronic information solutions system that can be immediately modified, updated, and changed as user information needs change. Third, it has one focus and one goal, and that is to provide

Winning the Information Game

the best real time information and insights possible to support user business profit and market goals.

Direct1's operations possess all the characteristics of a mature information clearing house, only they perform them across a number of different customer interaction dimensions. They maximize the immense power of the digital world to provide an ability to collect both question-driven and unstructured, comment-driven feedback. At the same time the internal structure of the clearing house is engineered to minimize the need for human intervention during feedback processing and analysis—sort of like the operation of a soda bottling plant. The human effort is concentrated at the input and output points with efficient monitoring of the intervening activities.

Instead of waiting for feedback to appear, as is the case with the USAA example, external clearing houses like Direct1 can also adapt to user needs "on the fly." If a user wants to change the feedback collection focus, that can be done in hours, with output displays also being modified accordingly. Should some piece of feedback be deemed especially critical to user business operations, then this feedback can be pushed forward for action immediately. This is a critical component for any clearing house operation to possess. Business information needs will never remain static, and it's nice when the user can count on the system to adapt to changing needs.

Backing everything up, Direct1 has a multi-faceted team of business experts who represent the different industries of user companies. By so doing, external clearing houses such as Direct1 add a new wrinkle to the clearing house function. By making it a business operation by itself, it provides the capability to import outside or inside benchmark feedback so users can also track themselves against their industry or other company metrics. Doctors intuitively do this when they view an EKG screen, looking for variations from the established norm. Now businesses can make use of this capability through external clearing houses. The following chart depicts generally how the Direct1 process works.

The most interesting aspect of an external clearing house is the fact that it is total and immediate, and the output displays can be

DIRECT1'S TOTAL FEEDBACK SYSTEM PROCESS

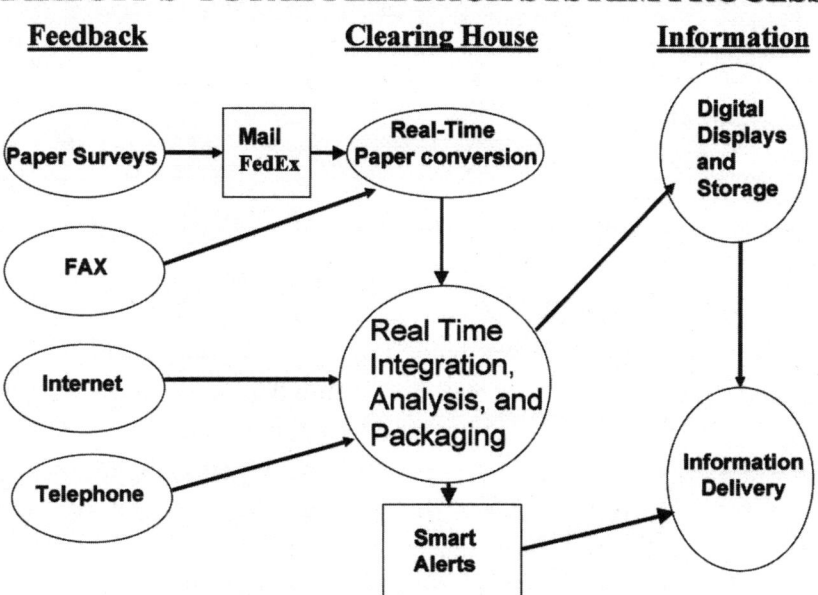

customized to support the entire business, from the CEO to frontline employees. Getting beyond the hype, it is clear that Direct1 understands that its job is to deliver the information the user wants. It steers clear of any pretense of trying to spin the output beyond the way the user wants it displayed. It is up to the user to place value on the information and have the will to act on it. Direct1 holds true to the most basic precept of successful clearing house operations—neutrality. Let the information do the talking.

THE APPLIED EXAMPLE—CSC HELP DESK

Today the matter of customer relationship management (CRM) is becoming much more than just a nice buzzword phrase. The speed of information age business operations demands that companies link ways to gauge customer reactions to their services, and products to their business metrics. To do anything else does not offer the prospect of really changing things or improving a business's competitive position.

Unlike a lot of other companies that talk about what needs to be done to achieve better CRM, Computer Sciences Corporation (CSC) is a company that acts. It decided it wanted to develop such tools through the use of real time external clearing house capabilities. Moreover, it wanted to do so in a fashion that not only improved its own operations but through public sharing of the results, demonstrated in a referenceable fashion how resulting information can be linked to performance metrics to improve CRM activities.

One point of friction with customers in companies historically has been Help Desks. CSC decided to team with Direct1 and create a Help Desk feedback system that provided a way to improve its own operations and demonstrate the power of an actual CRM tool when linked to performance metrics. The task was to engineer, place, and activate a real time external monitoring system within 60 days that allowed the Help Desk senior management to monitor on a continuous basis customer support, satisfaction, and problem resolution as a means of providing a business performance monitor and CRM tool for this critical activity.

All engineering and activation requirements were accomplished ahead of time. First, Direct1 knowledge engineers sat down with CSC Help Desk management to determine what information they needed in order to have an impact on the service and business metrics they were being measured on. At the same time, they determined how customers typically interfaced with the CSC Help Desk. In CSC's case, all interaction was by phone, but all customers had email addresses, so an electronic tracking ticket was created when they called in.

Once the knowledge-engineering phase was completed, Java-based feedback collection tools were created that would collect the feedback so that when processed it produced the information desired by the Help Desk management. These tools were then positioned so they could be accessed from CSC's Intranet or posi-

Deploying and Using Clearing Houses

tioned on the Internet in a way that customers could access them when asked.

The final step in creating the CRM feedback system was to create output screens that would display the processed information in useful ways to the CSC Help Desk management. Again, using an extensive library of available display options that used everything from trendline charts to carlike dashboard gauges, the Direct1 knowledge engineering team helped the Help Desk management decide on how they wanted the information displayed. Interestingly, bar charts were not in huge demand.

Finally, the whole resulting software package and system was stress tested. For the sake of a comprehensive test and to create a definitive metric-related baseline, it was decided that it was necessary to collect feedback from every customer who used the Help Desk for a period of 60 days. To make matters tougher, it was decided that the whole collection, processing and distribution clearing house operation would operate in a secure manner outside CSC's firewall. The results exceeded everyone's expectations. Managers began to improve not only the business metrics, but they discovered that the resulting information provided helpful hints that allowed them to anticipate potential problems. Further, they sped up the response to customer problems dramatically.

How did they achieve this result? The electronic ticket was the key. From it was stripped the information that allowed dispatch of an email to customers asking them for feedback and to click on a URL link embedded in the email. They were then taken to a site where, depending on the type of problem they had requested help with, they filled out an electronic java-based collection tool. Once it was completed, it was electronically sent through Direct1's electronic processing engine and the results posted on a display screen accessible to the Help Desk management. Activity is continuous, and displays reflect reactions to Help Desk actions within minutes of completion and closeout of the Help Desk problem ticket, giving management a real time view of what is happening in their Help Desk world.

Was the test a success. You bet! Today, CSC has a quality CRM tool that it can offer its users and partners. More important, CSC has a way to make significant and lasting process improvements in all its Help Desk operations on an immediate and continuing basis. Plus, the resulting data base can be used for follow up on analysis, and it is linked to other internal and external metrics for special monitoring. Finally, the system itself is structured so that it can be modified "on the fly" as CSC Help Desk information needs change.

LESSONS LEARNED

The examples just discussed offer several contrasts and insights. To complete the step of understanding, deploying, and using clearing houses, let me share several. The first lesson, again, is not to underestimate the impact of attitudes. There are a lot of negative feelings about feedback. We should not overlook them when getting serious about feedback. It was reported that USAA's clearing house found that the very word "feedback" struck fear into the hearts of many, because it was seen as a synonym for a complaint or embarrassment and more work.

In reality, those who wrote about ECHO™ reported that only about 30-40 percent of the information collected fell into this category. The remainder was great ideas from customers, compliments, suggestions for new products, and invaluable intelligence freely provided about competitors. However, it appears that the politics of trying to explain this to excited "in your face" managers can be a tall order.

Some call this problem the challenge of confronting company politics with an inside clearing house operation. Given that feedback operations depend on absolute neutrality of those working the feedback, the environment itself can remove that cover. The resulting politically charged atmosphere can act to retard the value of feedback developed and delivered by internal clearing houses by interjecting all sorts of "red herring" issues, such as loyalty and control.

In contrast, with the Direct1 example, the danger of internal politics is diminished. First, because Direct1 is divorced from internal company pressures, it can focus more completely on getting the

Deploying and Using Clearing Houses

information and leaving the interpretations and explanations to the user. Additionally, the user still retains the right to ignore or act on the information, whereas that is not always the case with internal clearing house operations. Finally, because Direct1 responds to information needs dictated by the user, control of what is gathered still remains where it belongs—with the information partner.

Regardless of whether the clearing house is inside or outside a business, the biggest challenge is to get people to view feedback positively and not go into spasms of fear and anxiety when they hear the word. While managers may report that they agree verbally with the words Every Contact Has Opportunity (ECHO™), under stress it appears people's actions sometimes say something else. In the case of Direct1 and outside clearing houses, just the fact that the information is coming in from somewhere else may cause misunderstanding and confusion.

If we decide to deploy clearing houses we must support them completely and make sure they are clearly tied to business goals and metrics. Here the CSC Help Desk example is instructive. By making sure the information distributed and fed back for action is clearly tied to business metrics, managers and users can see immediately the impact of the information to positively change things if they choose to do something with it. In this way CSC managers and managers in general are able to avoid the problem of becoming the lightning rod rather than being the problem solver.

Another insight offered by the three examples has to do with taking advantage of feedback opportunities. If the feedback efforts are primarily external in focus, then how do we take advantage of all the internally developed and stored information? It's the internal systems links where some other very significant payoffs can come, but it is also here where establishing the connections is the most difficult. In particular, the CSC example again demonstrates how one might approach the issue. The manager can take what the customers are feeding back on how the problem was handled and compare it with actual product data, thereby ensuring they have a complete qualitative and quantitative picture to help them with their problem solving-duties.

Winning the Information Game

In a slightly different way, external clearing houses have a similar but less complicated problem. When connecting to the user's systems, the external clearing house has only to worry about making a good link at that point. It becomes another systems loop that is integrated, but the user doesn't have to worry about maintaining it. However, once it begins passing information inside the partner company, an outside clearing house must also depend on the business's existing systems architecture and existing software.

For those of us who implement clearing houses, it would be prudent to work both external and internal information integration issues simultaneously. This can be called "engineering the information delivery capabilities," analogous to the biological mechanisms that regulate our body temperature. As one example, it might be prudent to engineer automatic marketing responses to be driven by preestablished and engineered information inputs. When developed, such feedback capabilities will free up resources for other tasks on an order that makes current reengineering efforts seem very small. One of the outputs of the CSC example is that managers are now able to develop customer-relations strategies for known recurring problems over which they have no control. Direct1's smart alerts are another example of what I am talking about here. They could be programmed to drive business responses if they were seen as critical.

Another insight! I suggested in the USAA example that manager and leader readiness to operate in an information-driven world is far more limited than we could have ever visualized. Frankly, I believe there is a huge employee skills gap that must be bridged across all business settings regardless of whether or not companies become effective at driving information. In fact, a lot of the negative attitudes that exist regarding the collection, aggregation and sharing of information can be traced back to a lack of skills.

In the past, managers everywhere were fed everything and mainly were accountable for results through application of templates. Analysts provided the numbers, seniors controlled and directed, and systems folks provided the templates. In the information age, we will have to do all these things and more ourselves

Deploying and Using Clearing Houses

without a lot of guidance, especially at senior executive levels. There won't be time for anything else. To survive, our companies will have to develop and implement programs to reduce the skill gaps at all management levels so everyone can develop a sustained ability to "read" things themselves.

For those who see cost as a major issue, we can make an argument that using an external clearing house is more cost effective. Without overstating things, it appears that USAA's internal operation is large and well financed. With an external clearing house, users can get the same information-leveraging power, but they don't have to worry about paying for the systems and people. It is a shared cost, and the more users, the cheaper the actual cost.

To adopt an "either/or" stance—either an internal or an external clearing house—is not the right solution. Rather, those desiring to drive information must realize that the optimum solution is probably an external and some sort of internal clearing house working together. External clearing houses optimize getting the right information to the right user very quickly. It takes internal clearing houses to make sure the right actions get taken and the information is shared. Attention will now be turned to some of the information operating principles that flow from all that has been discussed to this point. In turn, they serve as a prelude to a discussion of the companywide skills needed to become competent information drivers.

CHAPTER VI

INFORMATION GAME SUMMARY

Step IV (continued): Understand, deploy, and use information clearing houses

Establishing the internal clearing house.
- Organize with what you have—don't wait for the perfect solution.
- Tie all efforts to the core business vision.
- Have a clear plan and certain direction before you think about supporting systems.
- Focus clearing house efforts on promoting solutions and results. Don't move forward without top management support.
- Fix first, count and analyze later.
- Organize and orient to collect, collect, and promote action.

Using an external clearing house.
- Determine your information needs first.
- Engineer things so everyone who needs the information is included.
- Leverage the clearing house's speed.
- Continuously adapt its capabilities to changing information needs.
- Emphasize flexibility in all clearing house activities.
- Ensure that all clearing house information loops are linked.
- Be ready to do a lot of user training.
- Build a core electronic nerve network as part of the operation.
- Make sure all information systems are embedded in the operational fabric of the business.
- Be able to modify and adapt all clearing house systems easily. (Insights from the USAA, DIRECT 1, and CSC)
- Don't ever underestimate the power of attitudes.

Deploying and Using Clearing Houses

- Work to get people to view information positively.
- Develop both internal and external feedback capabilities together.
- Recognize and confront the information age skills gaps in managers.
- Tie information outputs to business metrics.
- Don't let cost blind you.
- Recognize that both external and internal clearning houses are probably necessary.

CHAPTER VII

KNOW THE INFORMATION PRINCIPLES

*"I am always ready to learn,
although I do not always like being taught."*
—Winston Churchill

Step five details the information principles we need to know and apply to win the information game. Knowing the principles serves to simplify many of the business tasks required for us to succeed and prosper in the information age. Applying them keeps us focused on the task at hand and away from side issues that can inhibit or confuse us about the proper application of our scarce company resources.

In this way we can avoid being like the new employee who found himself standing in front of the paper shredder looking confused. "Need some help?" a co-worker asked.

"Yes," the employee replied, trying to sound knowledgeable, "how does this thing work?"

"Simple," our helpful coworker said, taking the official looking report from his hand and feeding it into the shredder.

"Thanks, but where do the copies come out?"

Principle 1: Watch and Listen. This is the most obvious of the principles needed for us to be effective when acting to leverage and drive information; it is also probably the one least practiced and most often forgotten. We tell our people that good listening skills are the key to success. We admonish all within hearing to take time to listen and observe, but it has been reported that most of us spend the better part of our lives broadcasting rather than adhering to the principle of observing and listening. And for our companies, it's as if the increasing speed of information flow has blinded everyone to the enduring power of taking a step back to watch and listen.

The sad fact is that a failure to watch and listen can be downright dangerous and very self-defeating. For our companies it can be devastating. Business observers such as TARP report that a majority of our customers never tell our companies about their dissatisfactions. The customers who do take the time to give feedback are rarely heard because we are too busy writing surveys or hiring some consultant to figure out why customers are leaving. With the speed at which things happen in the information age, therefore, it is imperative that companies organize to watch and listen first.

A sad story that exemplifies the bottom-line cost that can result from not listening came from friends in the retail food business. An elderly customer had tripped while being assisted into the grocery store by her daughter. As she picked herself up, one of the workers asked if she was OK, and then as an aside to another worker, which the mother's daughter heard, commented that it looked like "Granny will live to trip another day." The daughter was incensed and demanded to see the manager. When he arrived, she told him she wanted an apology from the employee for his comment. Instead of getting the employee to apologize the manager, while appearing concerned, for some unknown reason didn't honor the request. The rest, of course, is history. For lack of listening and responding, the customers sued, and the store paid heavily.

Another friend had the misfortune of getting bad service at his favorite chain restaurant while visiting a large southern city on business. When the server failed to bring his coffee after the third

Know the Information Principles

request, he called the hostess over and asked to see the manager. When the manager came over, he told the manager about the problem and suggested that the employee get some training, as the oversight appeared to be a result of inexperience. The manager, rather than listening, informed my friend that he would get his dinner free.

"But I don't want a free dinner!" my friend replied.

"Well, that's the way we do it here," replied the manager, and off he went. My friend got up and left, saying to the hostess that this would be the last time he ever ate at this particular restaurant. The manager hadn't heard or realized that my friend didn't want a free dinner. He just wanted the server trained.

Principle 2: Be redundant. Business feedback is most useful when our company employs redundant active and passive forms to obtain information. The more we can cross reference multiple inputs, the more confidence we can have in the feedback we are receiving—sort of a built in "second opinion" capability.

In a biological sense, our sense of sight is wonderful, but I wouldn't want to try to make it on that one source of input alone. Imagine you are walking down a set of railroad tracks. Suddenly the tracks start vibrating. Then you hear a train whistle in the distance. You see the wisp of engine exhaust above the trees. Finally, you see the train. Regardless of how you got the feedback, by this time you should be off and well away from the train tracks. In fact, the key to the process of evaluating incoming data is to be able to respond the instant we receive enough corroborating input to conclude that a train is coming. Competent information-age companies must do the same if they are really serious about leveraging and driving information.

Principle 3: Act Simultaneously. Our companies must be able to do many things simultaneously if we are to meet the demands of operating in a feedback-rich world. As biological beings, we simultaneously acquire, analyze and respond continuously to a host of inputs. If there is any priority to our organic processes, it has to do with potential threats to individual or group survival. It seems the more critical the potential threat indicated by the

Winning the Information Game

information input, the more automatic our personal response. Therefore, our companies must also be in a constant state of simultaneous acquisition, processing, and responding. As business people, however, our goal is effective action in the service of our shared company vision.

In the past, our watchwords have been "sequential action." We see. Then we analyze. Finally, we act. That possibility still remains as an option, but now we are in a world that requires that we do more than one thing at a time. In fact, we need to be able to see, analyze, and act simultaneously. Therefore, establishment of priorities and defaults takes on new meaning. That is, our companies, like our bodies, must institute ways to be able to perform more than one function at a time. This capability is the key to speedy customer recovery or rapid responses to moves of a competitor.

A good example of this principle was shared with me by a business friend during a boring presentation at a conference we were attending. In front of him was his laptop. In his pocket was his cell phone. On his belt was his pager. As the speaker droned on, he worked on a report he was preparing. At one point, he made a call in response to a vibrating page. Then he took a call from his wife about an issue at home. Meanwhile, around us half the audience was asleep. He glanced around and said, "Look these poor souls. They don't have a clue that their snooze is probably the most expensive thing they've done today! You've got to stay connected all the time and be able to do more than one thing at a time to get ahead in business today!"

Principle 4: Change the Action Order. Fix first, count and analyze later. This principle, discussed briefly in a previous chapter, now deserves detailed treatment, for it establishes a new action order. In our biological world, certain responses about external inputs are established to promote immediate reactions without apparent thought—sweating to cool one's self, for example. To act otherwise could threaten our survival. After the danger has passed, the input can be counted and analyzed, and action priorities revised if necessary. Maybe I shouldn't have worn my sweats into the steam room!

Know the Information Principles

While it may seem to be a business contradiction to us, changing the action order to "fix first" actually serves to make subsequent counting and analyzing more effective. Analysis and pondering issues still count. That is the way we make sure we aren't doomed to fix the same thing time and time again. But now, instead of working in a vacuum, supporting business analysts, researchers, and planners have a context for what it is they are trying to do with the things they count and analyze.

They may even know some of the actions taken in response to information inputs. Business recommendations provided to us by researchers necessarily can now act to improve what may be temporary fixes, turning them into even more lasting systems improvements and business learning. They will no longer be reporting on things that have been overcome by other events because of the lengthy nature of the classic research process.

Principle 5: Develop a Business Focus. We are bombarded with a constant stream of sensory feedback. But we don't get overwhelmed. The reason is that we have a perceptual screen that serves as a protective, normally confusion-resistant barrier, letting things through only when certain learned intensity or uniqueness levels are exceeded. Our businesses need to deploy the same sort of capability with the use of redundant sources of feedback. This is the principle of business focus.

We need to develop the business focus screens in advance so we can ignore the rest of the business noise that goes on constantly. Given the criticality or business risk represented by the input, screening level for the business focus screens could and would vary. Here the key is knowing what kinds of feedback are critical and needed. There is an acronym for these kinds of critical indicators used commonly in intelligence gathering operations: EEI—essential elements of information.

As introduced in chapter four, in advance of deploying our interactive and redundant collection assets, we must, in accordance with our company's shared vision, determine what the essential elements of information are that we want to pay attention to. That is, what are the answers we want? Only in this way will we be able to deploy an effective collection screening and information acquisition capability. More important, only in this way can feedback reliability and usefulness be assured. Or to put it in plain business language: only in this way will we know what questions we want to ask.

As in all activities, there is a risk when we become selective, but we should not forget the power of focused effort. We can always change the focus if the need arises. Our selective business focus should enable flexibility, not become a tool of rigidity.

Principle 6. Keep Information Visible. If anything has characterized hierarchical organizations, it has been the idea that information is power and is to be guarded at all costs by each business stovepipe. Information still qualifies as power, but the information age has turned the idea of internal hoarding and hiding information on its ear. In some cases, it also makes keeping information from the marketplace counterproductive. Here, for example, I mean not making public feedback about our products and services. Because of the perishable nature of information and the speed with which it changes, particularly within our companies, we should take steps to make sure all information is pooled and available for everyone's review and use. To fragment business information so that only those in one small part of our business can use the information is tantamount to terminal business incompetence in the information age. At the same time, we cannot forget that we need to continue to protect from outsiders information that gives us those great product and service ratings as well as our competitive advantage.

I am reminded of a story told me by a marketing officer in a large pharmaceutical company about the moves a competitor was intending to make and how his company missed a great opportunity. The company planners got wind of the move but wanted to wait for a big corporate meeting to show their plan to counteract the move. They didn't share their knowledge with anyone, nor did they coordinate and see what other information might be available. The result, predictably, was chaos, a lost opportunity for the company's stockholders and a bottom line that suffered needlessly. Sadly, stories like these remain the norm and will probably end up as epitaphs on a number of corporate tombstones as long as egos are more important than the information that drives the bottom line.

Moreover, you learn a lot sitting beside people at conferences. While the speaker was delivering his message, I couldn't help but notice the agitated behavior of the person next to me. She kept searching through the pockets of her suit as if someone had deposited something there but had forgotten to tell her. "Can I help you?" I asked in a very tentative fashion.

"Certainly not!" she responded in a less than friendly way. Looking down, I noticed a piece of paper on the floor and bent down to pick it up. She snatched the paper from my hand. "How dare you!" she admonished me. "That's privileged information! I was worried"—and she gave the name of a person I neither knew nor had ever heard of—"that our planning representative had gotten a hold of the message my marketing VP had sent me. If she had, I would have been in deep trouble!" How sad! How typical!

The reality, in our electronic, information-rich world, like that of our biological sensory world, is that information has some value to almost everyone inside our businesses. So there is greater value to sharing than to hoarding. To sequester or hide information from others in our businesses diminishes the likelihood that timely actions will result, business learning will take place, or that we will achieve the ends we seek. Those who benefit from the behaviors of hoarding are actually those who put their business at risk in the information age.

Principle 7. Share. Information visibility helps improve things, but it depends on sharing for real power. The toughest thing for us to come to grips with in the information age is to realize that information sharing within our companies is critical to competitive success. For far too long information has been considered a commodity of political exchange. Inside old industrial-age companies it has been bartered for advantage, position, and even intracompany advantage.

The information age has drastically changed the equation. The only thing left to us is the certainty that the external environment can't be managed unless there is an unbeatable sense of internal unity. Internal disharmony, particularly that driven by information hoarding, brings defection, distrust, and turnover, which defeat any possibility of coherent progress or response to external challenges.

Internal sharing of information, despite the risk of exposure to external threats, builds a sense of ownership and involvement among our teams, departments, and people. Combined, these attributes serve to help build the business unity necessary to succeed. I ask: Why do internal agencies not share information? If the answer is that other members of the team can't be trusted or the information is too valuable, then I question the ability of that business to succeed. In fact, as bosses we just have to grin and bear it sometimes, and be just like the boss who asked one of her younger employees, "Do you believe in life after death?"

The employee promptly responded, "Yes, I sure do."

"Well then that makes everything just fine," the boss went on. "About an hour after you left yesterday to go to your grandfather's funeral, he stopped by to see you!"

Principle 8. Package for Use. Remember the discussion in chapter four about the importance of integration and processing things rather than just passing feedback through? This principle deals with the fact that all feedback, once it is processed, must be packaged for our use. This is done by either a clearing house (some group charged with pulling things together) or through embedded electronic (integration) packaging tools such as Direct1 uses in the example of an external clearing house. Just as customers have a number of ways they can interact with our companies, those of us inside have preferred ways we like to receive information. The better the packaging, analysis, and internal interface, the more meaningful and useful the information. Therefore, our goal must be to promote the recipient's ability to generate immediate solutions and results from the application of information.

Successful information-age companies will perform their key packaging functions through a number of information clearing houses. These clearing houses will draw on information warehouses that store external and internal data. Within these clearing

Know the Information Principles

houses, a number of analytic capabilities will be located. They will provide both automated and ad hoc processing and analysis for company customers. Once this is completed, the information is packaged against the essential elements of information (EEI) that have been established for the type of information the clearing house is collecting and distributing.

Senior decision makers, marketers, planners, and anyone else who needs the information will draw on these clearing houses, and there will be a new sense of priority and order to company information. In turn, all members of our company team will have to know more than just their share of the business process and be able to leverage what is coming to them from various integrative clearing houses. The principle of packaging, however, cannot be achieved unless we adhere to the next principle.

Principle 9. Use Facilitators. Specifically there are three types of information organizations: real teams, virtual teams, and systems teams, led by a new breed of company professionals who oversee things for us. Rather than being controllers and managers, these professionals are facilitators. Their competencies are a multi-disciplinary blend of technical, statistical, and humanistic systems. A facilitator's effectiveness is judged by his or her ability to integrate and facilitate the human, business and electronic worlds of the three types of information organizations that populate our emerging information-leveraged and -driven companies.

Real teams are the people who take specific inputs, package them, and then get the information to the right area for action. Then after ensuring action is facilitated, they perform their counting and analyzing activities. Sometimes they facilitate action themselves by managing an automatic transmission system which ensures that information is passed to the impacted area before it is counted and analyzed. Other times, they may take raw input, such as that received from customer surveys, analyze it, and then pass it to an area for action.

Virtual teams are responsible for taking information and acting on it. Sometimes they accomplish their responsibilities by direct response to the information received. Other times they may work in

Winning the Information Game

a cooperative fashion, sharing insights and solutions to similar problems with other parts of the company. Finally, virtual teams may put their heads together to work a problem that is new or is so widespread that it requires a group solution. The unique thing about virtual teams is that while separated, team members act as one when it comes to their responses to information received for action.

"Systems teams" refers to those who support by managing the electronic networks and infrastructure, inside or outside the company, established to facilitate the entire process. Some are analytic and focus on detailing trends, a sense of the criticality of the information, or a feel for the scope of the information. Other supporting systems functions are facilitative, because they allow users to store, and track actions taken and share the results. Still others are communicative because they allow those of us using the systems to collate, modify, share, and actually respond to information being transmitted. Regardless of whether or not a particular type of information organization is being used, they are the critical, generally human parts of the business, yet we tend to take them for granted. Therefore, I suggest to others that they lead and care for their real teams, support cross-company virtual teams, and manage supporting systems teams that wire everything together. If we do that, I promise, the hardware will take care of itself.

Principle 10. Reward. Typically when we are confronted with information that requires action, our first impulse is to view things negatively. If our companies are to drive and leverage information, we need to get beyond this attitudinal problem. It is destructive, as exemplified by the fine art of finger pointing, shooting the messenger, and ignoring the information. The solution for us is to accentuate the positive and reward, reward, reward. One very effective use of reward is to give points or performance bonuses to teams, departments, and individuals who initiate or take action on the information they receive. The points in turn are traded in for merchandise or gift certificates and the bonuses used as our employees wish.

Of course, there are lots of other ways we can reward people, but it is rare that companies systematically count and connect rewards to activities that foster fixing things and support vision accomplishment. More likely, rewards get attached to the personal interests of our boss. That's not necessarily bad if they are the same as our company's vision. Unfortunately, this doesn't always happen. As a result, rewards are often very inconsistently applied. Just as with the establishment of priorities for information collection, our companies need to be willing to put a reward priority on what they want done with the information distributed for action.

Principle 11. Link Feedback Loops. The final principle brings us full circle. As the following figure suggests, today's information flow is really a circular feedback process whose payoff centers on solutions and results. In contrast, in industrial age companies the model was linear. Or more important, it was personified by the fine art of "passing the buck." How many times have we heard the phrase "An action passed is an action completed"? Sadly, this way of thinking presumes that our actions will not come back to haunt us, which we know to be a faulty conclusion.

INFORMATION FEEDBACK LOOP

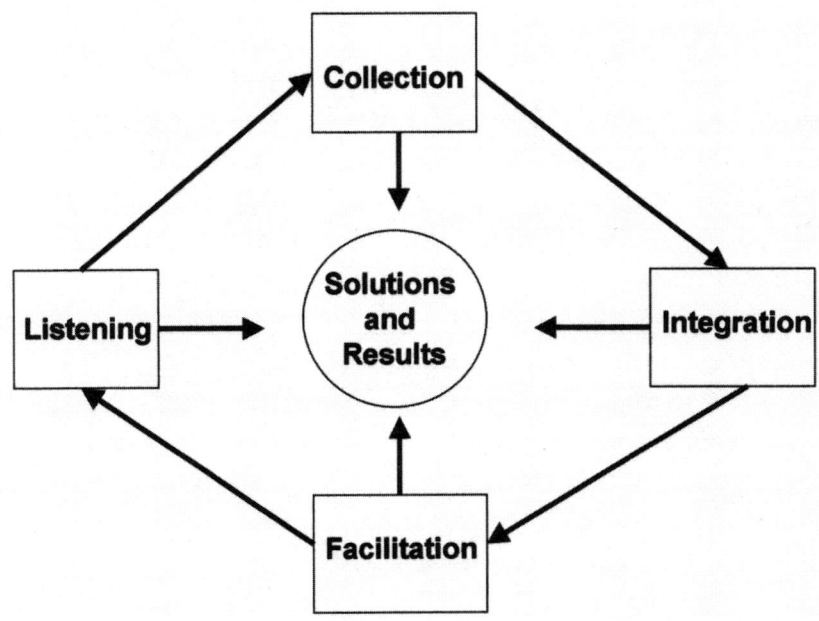

Across the company our real task is to link feedback loops so that an interactive, sharing whole is created. Again a biological illustration is useful. Internally, we are composed of a number of feedback systems, the circulatory and nervous systems, to name two. Their actions are circular, but they are linked and complementary. They feed off of one another and are helped by the integrative assistance of the brain and the automatic embedded neural nodes.

If learning is to take place, information flow must be essentially circular; otherwise there is no linking and no opportunity for feedback. It is a mystery to me why we have tended to see business relationships as a linear hands-off process. "Here, this belongs to you! I am now free and no longer accountable!" Maybe because things moved a lot slower in the heyday of the hierarchical organization, we could get away with such foolishness—not so any more. Our companies will roll into the future on feedback loops, not on open-ended linear functions. Our view of the flow of information must change from a linear one to a circular one. Only in this way can the chances for the lessons to be learned increase and our companies and our employees become adaptive users of information.

THE PAYOFF

Just knowing that the information principles are useful, because they provide the conceptual framework for better business thinking, is not enough. To stop there misses the point. The payoff is in their application. And application depends on skill. The following story is a good example of the importance of following through on feedback and applying sound operating principles. A complaint letter was received by the division president of a large car company. It read as follows:

"Dear Sir, this is the second time I've written you. I don't blame you for not responding, because I must sound half crazy, but I assure you what I am saying is true. We have a tradition in my family that we have ice cream for dessert every night. We vote on the kind we want, and then I drive to the store to buy it. It's also a fact that we just purchased one of your cars. The problem is that every time I buy vanilla ice cream, when I come back to the car

Know the Information Principles

from the store, it won't start. It doesn't happen with any other kind of ice cream. I'm beginning to believe we have a car that doesn't like vanilla ice cream, and that just won't do."

The division president had his doubts about the letter, but felt that if it was important to the customer, it ought to be important to him, so he sent an engineer to check things out. The engineer was pleasantly surprised to be met by a successful, obviously well-adjusted man. The engineer arranged to meet him after dinner, whereupon they hopped into the car and drove to the ice cream store. That night the order was for vanilla ice cream, and sure enough, the car wouldn't start when they came out of the store. Our engineer, not to be stumped, came back on several other occasions and the result was always the same when the flavor chosen was vanilla.

Surely they weren't dealing with a car that was allergic to certain flavors of ice cream. He stayed on the case and finally got a clue: It took less time for the man to buy vanilla ice cream. Because it was the most popular brand of ice cream, the vanilla flavors were kept in a case at the front of the store. The long and short of the story was that the car didn't have time to cool down. There was a short, and the electronics were not resetting. Well, they fixed the problem. The company now had a customer for life, and the day for the arrival of the human-machine had been postponed again.

The moral of the story is that where business information is concerned, even the most insane-looking problems are sometimes real. Following good information principles made a hero out of the division president, but his skill at seeing the relevance of the information and applying the information principles to win the game was really what got the process rolling. Let us now move to the next logical step, discussing the information skills we need to possess if we are to win and dominate.

CHAPTER VII

INFORMATION GAME SUMMARY

Step V: Know and act on critical
information principles

Driving information principles:
- **Watch and listen.**
- **Be redundant:** collecting information from multiple channels.
- **Act simultaneously:** acquiring, analyzing, and responding to a host of information inputs at the same time.
- **Change the action order:** fix first, count, and analyze later.
- **Develop a business focus:** discriminate between information inputs.
- **Keep information visible:** information must be available for everyone's use.
- **Share** the internal sharing of information builds a sense of ownership and involvement among teams, departments, and units.
- **Package for use:** information must be analyzed and packaged so it can be used quickly.
- **Use facilitators:** leverage the power of real teams, virtual teams, and systems teams to make information work for the company.
- **Reward:** use incentives to foster the use of information to fix things.
- **Link feedback loops:** the information process is circular not linear, and the payoff is solutions and results.

In general:
- Never forget to link your information feedback means together.
- Always establish in advance of operations the essential elements of information (EEI) you want to collect.
- Train and develop managers and leaders who can lead real teams, support virtual teams and manage systems.

CHAPTER VIII

POSSESS THE NEEDED SKILLS

*"It is possible to fly without motors,
but not without knowledge and skill."*
—Wilbur Wright

In our haste to win, we sometimes forget to take the steps necessary to equip ourselves with the needed skills. Or, we want to try something new, but don't, because we feel unprepared. The results can be both humorous and sad at the same time. We're often like two landscape workers who were digging holes just to fill them back in again. When asked what they were doing by an inquisitive observer, the two responded, "Oh we're planting trees, but the guy who normally puts the tree in the ground is sick today. We never learned how to do the planting so we're just doing what we always do."

If we want to drive the process and make information do our bidding, we must get beyond this kind of behavior. Sadly, I see, and am told, about landscape worker kinds of behavior all the time. Such reports come from business colleagues who are trying to improve their company's ability to do things faster and better but can't seem to get the "good ship *Enterprise*" to shift to doing the new things required to make it happen.

When the conversation inevitably gets to the details of some new process, for example, their tone abruptly shifts. Talk becomes punctuated with phrases such as "If only we understood how to use that software!" "What you just described is nice, but do you mind if I get one of my systems people to give you a call? I'm too busy running my operations!" "My secretary handles all my email and office automation—I just use the computer when they want to show me something."

Some have even suggested that we resort to a technique a young business person had to use with her parrot. She had been given the parrot, full grown, with a bad attitude and a vocabulary to match. Every other word out of the bird's mouth was a cuss word, and it was a rude and nasty bird to boot! She tried everything in order to improve the parrot's vocabulary and attitude, from saying polite words to playing soft music.

Nothing worked. She yelled at the bird, and it would yell back. She shook it and it would bite her and squawk all the louder. One day in a fit of anger and desperation, she threw the bird into her freezer. For a few moments she heard the bird squawk and scream, then suddenly all was silent. Fearing she might have hurt the bird, she opened the freezer door. The parrot calmly stepped out onto her extended arm and said, "I do believe I have offended you with my rude behavior! I promise from now on to correct my behavior. I am truly sorry and beg your forgiveness." She was astonished to see the sudden change and was about to ask why when the parrot continued, "May I be so bold as to ask what the chicken did?"

FRAMING THE PROBLEM

We don't want to be like the parrot, but it is no wonder many of us feel left out and overwhelmed. The information age is passing us by as we sit in meetings or go about the industrial age business of controlling, directing and being driven by information. If we had the skills to tune in an hour or so a day to the electronic world around us, we would be amazed at what we could learn, and our companies would be far more productive places. A new employee and customer cyberworld inside and outside our busi-

Possess the Needed Skills

nesses has appeared before our very eyes. And it just doesn't stop with computers. I am including other mediums, such as intelligent phone systems, the fax, and interactive television. Therefore, just as information availability has proliferated, so too has the need for new information-age skills at all management levels. To succeed, we must bridge the gap now!

Usually, but mistakenly, the answer to the skills problem is inevitably framed as being one rooted in human relations issues. "All we need is better, more caring leadership." Describing the attributes of the environment desired is certainly useful, but backing up and underpinning every attribute must be the presence of real skills. For starters, without skills to interface with the digital information world that now surrounds us, the chance of fostering effective change or action is limited at best.

Cheerleading, hype, and manipulation—the tools of choice for substitute training activity—have always been an invitation for trouble. They tend to politicize the entire process. In the information age such activity invites business chaos, especially when it may be a result of the application of the wrong skills caused by the wrong focus. Remember, the only things that really matter when we are competing are action, solutions and results. If we succeed, self-esteem, positive feelings, and a sense of accomplishment will follow.

Abraham Zaleznik noted in a recent reprint of his classic *Harvard Business Review* article entitled "Real Work" that process and politics often get more attention today than products, markets, and customers. Put another way, organizations put interpersonal matters ahead of the things a business needs to do to succeed—real work! We may profess belief in a business vision that defines the work needed to be accomplished; but in practice, our actions, solutions, and results are activities that may make people feel good but take the focus away from doing the needed work.

The need for real, digital-world work skills is clear, particularly when we look at the skill-development curriculums of most management and executive development programs. They are replete with soft skills, such as leadership enhancement, conflict resolution, introspection, and self-assessment. Soft skills have their place, but where are the leader courses on organizational development, product management, computer literacy, digital systems operations, and information integration and analysis. How can we focus on real work if we don't have the real skills to do so in the first place?

As if to confirm the problem, Zaleznik observes, "Of course process and procedures are important, . . . but process and procedures are not the substance of business, and they should not get as much attention as, or more attention than, the work of business itself."

SURVIVAL SKILLS

Getting the real work done depends on one thing. We and our employees must have the skills to leverage the potential of the new digital tools available today and then cope with the speed of resulting business actions. We can never predict accurately which skill or skills may be important. Certainly, none of us is capable of being strong in every business skill, but we can become knowledgeable enough to be good in some and adjust our actions in others where we are weak.

In this way, we will avoid being like the young businessman who had just started his own business. He had set up a beautiful office and had it furnished with the best looking furniture he could find. As he sat admiring things, a visitor came into the outer office. Wanting to play the role of the big shot, he picked up the phone and made like he was closing a big deal. When he finished he motioned to the visitor and asked, "Can I help you?"

Without cracking a smile, the man replied, "Sure, I've come to hook up your phones." The survival skills that will facilitate business coping and our ability to leverage the power of the information age fall into three skill groups: relationship skills, facilitation skills, and analytical skills.

RELATIONSHIP SKILLS

Let's look at relationship skills first. No, I'm not contradicting my earlier comments about business's tendency to overemphasize these behaviors. They are always part of the equation. Remember, however, this is a discussion about the need to shift our focus, sets,

Possess the Needed Skills

and paradigms. We also need to shift our view of the concept of relationships as a needed skill set for the information age. The new definition we need to learn to define relationship skills is simple. Relationship skills refer to the abilities of managers and business professionals at all levels to see relationships between business functions and then leverage those insights for competitive advantage by acting on how the business parts—systems, organization, and people—fit and work together.

A while back, I took a three-day course about how to use an advanced slide-show and chart-creation program known to most as Microsoft Power Point. Some of my associates wondered somewhat humorously if I wasn't moving backwards rather than forward in my career-development skills. "How can such a program benefit you? That's tech/secretary work," they observed somewhat critically.

"What happens when you are on the road and you want to change your presentation because of new information?" I asked. "Who are you going to call?" The point here is that while I may not create the slide presentation, I had better know enough about the software so I can use it to make some changes.

It may fall to one of our systems people to know all the details of a system, but for a business system to succeed, business professionals must know the concept and how it relates to other systems. Further, they must appreciate and understand the strengths and weaknesses of the systems that support their business activities. Some practice and experience are necessary, but more important is the skill of understanding how all the systems fit together—seeing the relationships.

Tell me now, where are the business professionals today who can do this? Remember, the technical experts don't count here. If I want to have this phone, computer, or software system support some business strategy, how does a change in one system impact the other systems? Leave it to the experts, you say. Balderdash! Understanding systems relationships is a needed business skill for the information age!

Turning to organizational relationship skills, the need is no less critical. Those of us who understand set disciplines, such as plans or marketing, are everywhere. Where are the people who have the skills to understand how to adapt differing organizational structures to address situational changes that typically cross organizational turf boundaries? For the most part, they don't exist.

Still, today we must turn to industrial age stovepipes, such as Human Resources or Organizational Planning for assistance. Observers of the business world suggest that to reorganize a unit takes around three months. To change a department takes a year. Who knows what it takes to change a company, given all the internal politics? The bottom line is that this skill needs to exist across our businesses, with successful action decentralized and results measured in days. Until we as management have the skills to understand organizational relationships, it won't happen. We need to ask all those well-meaning business schools—Who is teaching this skill? And what are we doing to develop our own skills?

This brings me to the final aspect of relationship skills, the human domain. Here we need to bring to bear activities that promote what Abraham Zaleznik means by "real work." Any focus on human factors that does not support real work is not functional. Businesses exist as entities to do work first and as social groups second. Human relationship skills that foster a focus on results and productivity are good. Other focuses are at best a luxury and a secondary outcome. Four human relationship skills are key: perspective, teaching/coaching, listening, and interpersonal.

1. Perspective Skills. Perspective skills allow us to rise above detail and view customer, competitor, and employee situations in their entirety. With them we look at an event or an opportunity and contrast its present utility with its long-term human resource importance to the company's goals to establish its relevance. Perspective skills are based on our appreciation for the capabilities of our employees and a conceptual ability to relate their current capabilities to future needs to service customer and competitor demands.

Those of us who lack appropriate perspective skills typically pursue short-term goals without regard for long-term consequences. We emphasize form over substance. Here I'm talking about pushing something we think the boss wants rather than what the work or vision requires. We counsel the expedient at the expense of what is correct. Again, what does the work situation demand versus what do we need to do to get the boss off our back and get along? Our effect is to cause our departments and employees to lose their professional balance. What's more important, supporting an incompetent player or standing up for what is needed to win the business game and succeed?

When we do this we become dysfunctional politicians. Instead, we must be as quick as the experienced businessman who became exasperated with the beginner who kept pestering for a raise. He asked him why he kept asking for a raise when he had no experience. The beginner replied, "Work is very hard when you are a beginner."

"It becomes easier as you get experience," the businessman replied.

2. Teaching/Coaching Skills. Application of teaching skills is the means by which business professionals demonstrate that they care for their employees. The 1999 US Soccer World Cup Woman's team, winner of the Soccer World Cup, offers us a lesson here. The coach, as reported in most major newspapers, is quoted to have suggested that he coached his players as if they were men, but he treated them as if they were valued women. Only in this way can we as business leaders ensure that the procedures and actions we want emphasized are passed on to our employees. Teach them as if they were the one delivering, regardless of gender, but treat them with full regard for their gender. Teaching and coaching should not be delegated. When managers teach, they give meaning to the work of their companies and add value as leaders.

Those of us who possess good teaching and coaching skills emphasize informal teaching techniques over more formal means whenever possible. Further, whenever possible we accentuate the positive in our coaching approaches. Moreover, understanding the speed of information-age activity, we choose operational situations in which the lessons can be put to use immediately. Finally, when we are competent teachers and coaches, we make sure that our employees develop and practice good teaching skills, and our entire company constantly challenges itself to grow and develop. No management substitutes and no finger pointing are allowed. And we all work to find ways to celebrate and support business successes.

3. Listening Skills. Listening skills are vital as a relationship skill. To leverage the human power of our businesses, managers at every level need every bit of information they can get their hands on. But we forget that listening is a powerful and efficient way to accomplish this goal. In contrast, with well-developed listening skills, we recognize that it is the quality of listening that counts rather than the amount.

Understand that we must practice our listening skills to realize the benefit. In this way we become expert at developing business listening systems to hear what our customers and employees are telling us. Moreover, we are good at picking the right people to listen to. Further, we share what we learn. Next, we keep listening distractions to a minimum and refrain from interjecting our own biases and interrupting. Then we organize our own thoughts before responding.

4. Interpersonal Skills. Good interpersonal skills promote trust in our companies. Trust in turn acts to limit the procedures and rules required to foster action, solutions, and results. Further, interpersonal skills provide the confidence employees have in us because they force us to validate our commitment. Those of us who apply good interpersonal skills know our own biases, frustrations, ambitions, and desires, and work to avoid negatively influencing our business actions. Without effort, we avoid becoming like the nouveau-riche stock broker who splurged on a Rolls-Royce and decided to impress one of his more important clients, a very senior bank officer. He offered him a ride home one day and then couldn't resist asking, "Whaddaya think?" "Pretty classy, eh? I bet you've never ridden in one of these before."

"Actually, I have," his client graciously responded, "but this is the first time in the front seat."

The payoff for good interpersonal skills is immediate and profound. If we take the time required to maintain our interpersonal skills we will have employees who keep their focus on work goals and see us as caring leaders. The benefit we will see is an enhanced ability of our businesses to operate with a minimum of reliance on formal directive-driven systems and external control mechanisms.

FACILITATION SKILLS

As a skill group, relationship skills provide the base that sustains our personal requirement to act and get involved in the business process. In contrast, facilitation skills sustain our courage to motivate and challenge others to act in ways that promote business success. They provide us with the confidence to be flexible, the willingness to face change, and the ability to apply our relationship skills fully. Facilitation skills are the source of our professional business discipline.

Again, I think a humorous vignette puts things in perspective. A young MBA graduate applied to a finance company for a job, but he knew he had no experience. He was so intense that the accounts receivable executive gave him a tough account with the promise that if he collected it, he'd get the job. Two hours later, the MBA grad returned with the entire amount.

"Amazing!" the executive said. "How in the world did you do it?"

"It was easy," exclaimed our MBA grad. "I told them if they didn't pay up, I'd tell all their other creditors they paid us."

Both companies and the business world today are more complex. There are more conflicting requirements and options for us to consider in shorter periods of time. It is more difficult to make the necessary cause-and-effect linkages to act. Finally, it is impossible to influence directly all activities required for business success. To activate others, therefore, four facilitation skills are critical to our information age business success: endurance, risk taking, coordination, and persuasion.

Winning the Information Game

1. Endurance Skills. Why is endurance a facilitation skill? Take a look at all the stress and disease present in our business worlds today, and the answer is self-evident. Sick people are destructive and a drag on companies. More directly, the ability to be present at critical places and times, look to the well-being of employees, and teach and encourage people depends on solid endurance skills. Only with endurance can we maintain patience, a sense of humor, and perspective while sharing the fears and frustrations of our employees.

Endurance skills have two components—physical and mental. Business challenges demand men and women who have strong bodies as well as strong minds. It is time that this need be recognized, practiced and rewarded by everyone. As a facilitation skill, endurance does not demand that business leaders and managers maintain the ability to out-muscle their employees; rather, it requires continuing attention to physical and mental conditioning. Without this conditioning they will be unable to withstand the wearing effects of the unrelenting stress and strain caused by information-age business operations.

2. Risk-Taking Skills. As a facilitation skill, risk taking may also seem misplaced. Consider this fact: If you as a business person aren't ready to risk something in support of company goals and objectives, then who will be? And how will you motivate others to risk? Only by taking reasonable risks can our businesses hope to succeed. At the same time, prudent business professionals know that risks are purposeful decisions made carefully; they are not gambles.

In the digital information age where the action cycle is compressed, risk is a certainty. There is never enough time or enough resources to cancel out risk. Further, there is never any guarantee of success. As a facilitation skill, risk taking does not limit the fact that risk exists. Instead, it makes the reality of risk an opportunity and a reason to motivate others, knowing that our competitors have to contend with the same difficulties.

3. Coordination Skills. Coordination skills are my favorite facilitation skill because our companies apply them so poorly.

Coordination skills are activities designed to enhance the ability of the different parts of our businesses to work together. At lower levels, they are focused on activities that promote interplay, sharing, and teamwork. At middle levels of our companies they promote efficient application of resources and human effort. At senior levels, they promote our ability to communicate the problems, positions, and image of our companies, externally, as well as to our businesses as a whole, so that our activities receive the necessary support. Recently *Fortune* magazine published a piece which suggested that as a group, CEOs had a lot to learn about being good coordinators and willing sharers. What I think was being suggested is that the old model of the CEO as a loner is a concept with a limited future in the information age.

Without exception, coordination skills minimize chaos and confusion when they result in companies whose teams and departments are a beautifully interlocked whole, possessing an unshakable unity of purpose. This promotes and motivates all of us to demonstrate goal-directed, cooperative, understanding business behaviors. The impact on our competitors is an unbeatable business with class and staying power.

4. *Persuasion Skills.* When added together, all facilitation skills serve to reinforce application of the final skill—persuasion. The most effective way to deal with external or internal resistance endemic to all our business activities is to apply well-developed persuasion skills. However, there is a risk because, incorrectly used, persuasion becomes manipulation. What is the difference? Manipulation is the devious application of influence without sharing our reasoning and intent. It subverts initiative, is power-based, and is without moral direction. Its effect is to destroy the unity and cohesion of our business action. Further, it relies on appeals to the person as opposed to a focus on the work needing attention.

In contrast, persuasion depends on a willingness for us to be open about our aims and goals. This includes actions that include group involvement, work-focused motivation, sharing of the details, and management accountability. Being open about aims and goals ensures that our teams understand what is desired. Involving

Winning the Information Game

all the groups impacted promotes early tabling of all issues and unleashes the power of creativity. Work-focused motivation engenders common focus, a positive outlook, and cooperation, and promotes ownership and feedback to everyone involved. It occurs when we are willing to commit ourselves to the work that needs to be done, roll up our sleeves, and lead to motivate others. The result is truly a common focus. Finally, management accountability ensures that those of us directing an action are part of the team, have a better sense of the risks, and are willing to live with the outcomes.

ANALYTICAL SKILLS

The final set of information-age business survival skills we need are the value-added personal capabilities that we ourselves bring to the business process. Strong analytical skills are much more than the adept handling of numbers. Strong analytical skills allow a person to be inferential and creative, seeing insight, not numbers. I tire of the times that I have seen people who worry about the numbers rather than the insights. Frankly, analytical skills are our first line of defense when dealing with information-age complexity, allowing us to shape the future, be proactive, and generate the capability to out think our competitors. Four analytical skills are vital to our capability to add value: assessment, decision making, forecasting, intuition.

1. Assessment Skills. Assessment skills are important because they provide us the focus to determine the condition of our departments, teams, and companies. Properly developed, assessment skills allow us to collect and use information that enable our companies to be self-correcting and self-renewing.

Assessment and the generation of its associated numbers can produce useful insights if we do not get blinded by the numbers. Statistics, properly understood, can inform, educate, and motivate. Conversely, statistics, if misinterpreted, can cause business and team frustration, misinformation, and ethical dilemmas. As a very insightful and skilled senior business professional once told me, "Always work the numbers until you make them talk!"

Possess the Needed Skills

To apply assessment skills, first determine the need and benefit of undertaking an assessment. Then determine the use for the results of the assessment. Is it to review the company's ability to execute a business strategy? Or is the need to evaluate the adequacy of supporting business systems? Last, clearly communicate to teams and departments the reasons for use of an assessment.

2. Decision-making Skills. In contrast to assessment skills, decision making is a difficult analytical skill for us to master. At the same time, it is the most important analytic activity we perform for our businesses. Application of decision making establishes accountability and responsibility, even though decisions are always based on incomplete and sometimes inaccurate information. Moreover, it involves empowering our employees so that good decisions are made at all the right levels. Finally, its quality determines the trust and commitment that employees will have in us to carry out the decision.

Two activities are essential to good effective decision making—synthesis and analysis. As part of good decision making, synthesis makes the seemingly complex and disorganized meaningful and useful to our companies. Data are collected and matched with other data until the pieces fit, like a mental jigsaw puzzle. Information is combined with other data or information in the same manner. At this point, the result is processed information that can be transmitted, analyzed, or packaged to promote actions that foster solutions and results.

Conversely, our ability to analyze effectively is important because it provides the framework within which we view information, attach importance to it, determine its relevancy to our business or competitive situation, and then make a decision. Good analysis allows us to take information apart rapidly, establish patterns, and construct the necessary business priorities for our current or future action.

Having said all this, effective decision making skills are uniquely personal in application. No two of us will apply them the same way. Therefore, we have to always guard against personal traits such as stubbornness, arrogance, or overconfidence that may bias our analyses and synthesis. Moreover, timing is critical because it limits confusion in fast-paced information-age business environments. Knowing when to make a decision or when to do nothing can be as important as the decision itself. Another mentor once told me, "Always look for the competitors who think they have found truth with a capital 'T,' and there you will find the makings of your next conquest."

3. Forecasting Skills. Forecasting refers to our skill of "reading" the numbers and forming a broad projection of what needs to be accomplished over extended periods to produce some business result. Forecasting is our aggregation of all available information formed to allow us to visualize ways that may lead to the desired outcome. Put another way, forecasting allows managers and leaders to think of today's actions in terms of tomorrow's needs.

At the top, strategic planning is a type of forecasting activity. Within our business units and departments, phased plans that provide direction and the ability to confront differing contingencies approximate forecasting. Finally, our quarterly goals and objectives for our teams and units are the result of forecasting. A CEO may think and forecast in years, while a business unit leader may forecast in months, and teams in days and weeks.

4. Intuition Skills. "Whatever we may think about the information age, it is new and different to me!" This comment from a member of a group I was speaking to highlights the importance of the final analytical skill—intuition. Without intuition skills, we will end up wondering what happened, because we won't have acted. Intuition skills come from those quick and ready insights that are the result of study of and concentration on the critical business issues we are facing. It's very hard but very critical creative work. It's that sudden flash of light that enables us to be creative and to find workable, original and novel solutions to business problems.

Master chess players exemplify to me good examples of people with exceptional intuition skills. Because of highly refined assessment, decision-making, and forecasting skills, they are able to rule out whole classes of moves and rapidly concentrate on the ones that offer the best chance of success. Isn't this the ultimate demand of the information age and our key to success? Shall we say that we can't win the game without this capability? You be the judge!

What chess players are actually doing is determining what options are not possible. Then they continue refining things until they are left with only one or two options that may work. Do we do this in our business analyses? Find me the business plan that contains the options which won't work. We do it rarely, if ever. Chess players then choose between the remaining options, confident that the chances for success are increased. Where uncertainty and chaos are endemic, as in our businesses, any activity that systematically rules out options automatically improves our chances for success. One of the greatest compliments I ever had was on recommending that we not do something. The senior executive said it was the first time he had ever sat through a briefing which recommended the business not act on a course of action being evaluated! He found this important and reassuring.

Can we point to any one of the three skill sets as more important? I would not! The art is in their application. In fact, in practice, using well-developed relationship, facilitation, and analytical skills together is always the most stable and practical solution. Their effectiveness can be likened to a three-legged stool. When all three legs are present, we have a stable and useful platform from which to launch and deal with the world. With less than three legs, the prospects are quite different. In fact, the results can be downright terminal. With that encouraging note, we are ready to take the final step and cover the information potholes we need to avoid as we drive down the information highway on our way to winning the information game.

CHAPTER VIII

INFORMATION GAME SUMMARY

STEP VI: Possess the needed information skills

- Caring leadership is important, but it's not the only key to information-age success. Success depends on hard skills that promote real work.

Information-driving skills fall into three groups: relationship, facilitation, and analytical.
- **Relationship skills** include perspective, teaching, listening, and interpersonal. Together they provide the base that sustains our desire to act. They also leverage insights about how the systems, organization, and people fit together for competitive advantage.
- **Facilitation skills** include endurance, risk taking, coordination, persuasion. Manipulation is persuasion gone haywire. These skills sustain our courage to motivate and challenge others.
- **Analytical skills** include assessment, decision making, forecasting, and intuition. They are value-added personal capabilities that allow you to get beyond the numbers, to infer, and to think holistically.

- No two business professionals will apply decision-making skills the same way.
- Increase your chance of success by first determining what is not possible.

CHAPTER IX

AVOID THE INFORMATION HIGHWAY POTHOLES

*"Any man who afflicts the human race
with ideas must be prepared to see
them misunderstood."*
—H. L. Mencken

At the beginning of this book I asked if you were tired of being pushed around by all the data and feedback cascading down on us. Now you are now ready to move forward to win the information game and dominate your markets. You've taken six important steps. You've won the battle within, realized the importance of a shared business vision, and you now understand and can solve the riddle of the three I's. Further, you appreciate the power of information clearing houses and are willing to deploy and use them, understand the principles required to drive information, and know what skills you need to possess to succeed.

Let's take the final step to win the game! We need to avoid a number of information potholes that dot the information highway as we move forward. The experience of those who have already grappled with the more perplexing challenges of information-age business operations can help us avoid hitting many of these potholes ourselves. It may be nice to get an "A" for effort at the end of an information-age business day, but it is hard to consider the effort successful if we are missing some of our critical business anatomy.

The truth of the matter is that unwise business behavior will always result in disaster, regardless of the age. The only difference is that today it will happen faster and more completely. Ten of the most critical information potholes are covered in the following pages. They are business practices we should avoid in any situation, at all costs. Sadly, they are especially destructive as we learn to cope with the new digital information-age rules.

1. Underestimating the impact of attitudes. We have talked a lot about attitudes in this book. I make no apology for that. As a pothole in the information age highway, underestimating the impact of attitudes ensures that we will always ascribe more positive motivations to business behaviors inside or outside our companies than is warranted or prudent. I'm reminded of Shakespeare's tragic heroes, who always seem to underestimate the attitudinal context of forces that are arrayed against them. In a current business sense, this ensures that our business actions will be subject to surprises and failures that could otherwise be avoided. Some of the attitudinal problems are driven by a lack of understanding and effective communications. Others are driven by plain old sabotage and self-interest. Finally, others spring from a fear of the new and different. Must we be damned to become a modern-day Shakespearean tragedy in the way our businesses choose to operate?

Regardless of the source of the attitude, we must always be aware of their existence, acting purposely and decisively to overcome their negative effects. Liberal leveraging of situations where we communicate, and then communicate, and then communicate again are absolutely vital. I'm not talking about broadcasting where things are one way. I'm talking about getting involved and talking with and listening to our employees, customers, and competitors, and then sharing with one another. Unfortunately, most of us stop the process when we are finished broadcasting or our ideas don't get accepted. We ignore the fact that getting involved promotes the necessary modification in our own actions, as well as

Avoid the Information Highway Potholes

those with whom we interact. While good communications have a human relations component that is positive, the reason for undertaking them is to promote better work outcomes!

Too often, groups—especially our employees and management—talk by one another. All that happens in these situations is that competing attitudes are reinforced and there is never closure or understanding. The predictable result is conflict and failure for both parties. I was visiting a large computer firm when the business unit manager shared an attitudinal problem that almost resulted in the failure of a new product launch.

The firm wanted to bundle a new computer with a vary reliable printer produced by another part of the company to enhance the prospect of a successful launch. To do so, a modification needed to be made to the printer so it could be mated with the computer. The employees who produced the printer were worried that taking the time to do so would result in a loss of sales of existing printers, and thus cause them to miss meeting the goal that drove their bonuses.

The employees producing the computer saw the other group as an impediment to their potential survival. It appeared that both groups might fail as a result of talking past one another. Then their managers got together and talked things out. The original goals remained, but they added an incentive goal for bundled products produced which depended on both groups sharing. The result was a transformation in attitudes, and all goals were met.

To put the problem in perspective, when driving information, there is always the potential of attitudinal push-back. Remember our discussion from chapters five and six on clearing houses? Just having a central group serving as a clearing house by collecting data, organizing it and then disseminating it is enough to drive old- style managers crazy. They feel they have lost control, are suspicious, and will act without hesitation to neutralize the perceived threat. Success is only possible when we deal with the attitudes and show them to be unwarranted. Going the extra mile to make sure receiving managers win with the information helps. But mostly, we just need to make sure that nothing is done without an appreciation and consideration for other business professionals' attitudes in advance of any action.

2. *Becoming the message rather than the messenger.* Disseminating the information that is collected and packaged always entails risk. To ensure that a message receives the appropriate attention there is always the temptation to deliver it with great fanfare and flourish. This does not constitute an effective act of driving information! In these circumstances, the focus can be moved from the message to the messenger, and we risk getting shot! In other situations, the message can be sent routinely. When disaster ensues, we can again become the target. "You should have alerted me to the potential problem!" How do we avoid such a fate?

For these reasons, it is important to have clear ground rules about how information should be shared. Firm accountability for what is to be done also is of value. But most important is keeping the message and the messenger separate as much as possible. To accomplish this, automating an information clearing house such as was done in the example of Direct1, using USAA's training approach, or keeping the information tied to corporate metrics as CSC does, can help.

Keeping the message separate from the messenger can be accomplished through extensive use of technology and a clear definition of the roles. Messengers are responsible for maintaining the systems that deliver the messages. They should not intrude in the problem-solving process unless it is to provide more information. They are facilitators only. Everything should be made as automatic as possible. The receiver or their agents are responsible for acting on the information and reporting results back, which are then passed to senior management or the rest of the company. Messengers should not correct receivers if they fail to hold up their part of the bargain.

In spite of such safeguards, messengers can still run the risk of getting their posteriors ventilated unnecessarily. In these cases the best defense is the absolute integrity of our actions and the ability to remain neutral. In addition, remaining absolutely dedicated to the message-delivery processes we facilitate further assists. Finally, we need to make sure we maintain the support of those who chartered our activities—the higher in the company, the better.

3. Allowing information to get personal. An enduring threat when acting to leverage and drive information is allowing the information to get personal. I'm referring to the time-honored activities of "finger pointing" and "blame placing." Remember that success in the information age depends on fixing things, finding solutions, and promoting results. While finger pointing may provide psychological relief and blame placing may shift attention, neither activity does anything to fix things, find solutions, or promote results. What it does do is destroy teamwork, promote distrust, and slow business actions. In situations where speed, harmony, and decisive action are a must, when we allow information to become personal, failure becomes a certainty.

As business professionals we must act diligently to keep the focus on tasks, problems, and things and not people. I asked the leadership of one company I spoke with regarding its very effective employee feedback program, why it required anonymity in all inputs. The reply was direct. The company wanted the focus on the problem and not the person. They found that when employees identified themselves, managers tended to grade the feedback based on the personality of the person sending the message. It blinded them to some very important gaps that needed to be addressed. A major failure that had been reported, but discounted because the employee was considered a below average performer caused them to realize their error. From that point on in the company, the focus shifted from the origin of the message to the message itself.

When I hear calls for the need to identify the sources of all information, I don't get concerned, but I am left to wonder. What does this really add if it's the message that's really important? Moreover, any good information aggregation and analysis program should contain cross-check provisions to allow verification of the feedback received. A sad but true story related to me illustrates the need to cross-check information.

Winning the Information Game

A very young and talented manager had just moved to a new department where, with one exception, those she managed and the bosses above her were new. One of her subordinates, through her spouse, knew the new boss above the manager. In the course of events, it became clear to the manager that her new boss was struggling to learn the job. In a staff meeting, the young, talented manager noted this, and in an attempt to be helpful she cautioned everyone to be extra careful and do their homework before presenting anything to the new boss. Well, the subordinate told her spouse about what had been said, and he in turn related back to the boss that the young and talented manager had questioned her judgment. Rather than investigating the context of things, the boss removed the manager, much to the detriment of all.

The moral of the story is an enduring one. When the source of our information is not a direct one, we always need to step back. Verifying before acting is always prudent, even in extremely fast moving circumstances. And if we will just overcome our own biases, those of us charged with fixing things will find we have the experience and the skill, if we have the will.

4. *Failing to embed information-gathering activities in the existing operational and organizational structure.* I was visiting with a business friend who worked for a large automobile manufacturing company. He was going on at length about its very impressive complaint and feedback processing center. I asked what the company did with the vast amount of data collected by the many people who worked in the center. After a period of silence, he admitted that they didn't do much. The organization had been created as a separate function outside the normal operating and administrative structure of the company. Customers had the 1-800 number for registering complaints, but there were no electronic connections to dealers, product developers, product managers, or management. What existed was a tool of great potential but one that was functioning like a very expensive black hole for information.

This situation is more the norm than the exception in our companies, and it needs to be avoided if we are to drive information and move forward on the information highway. Our businesses, like people, seek balance and comfort. However, when people go to great lengths to deny, delude, and ignore information needed to learn, grow, and change, they usually don't survive, or they end up in some institution. Companies, on the other hand, once they have established themselves, seem to go to great lengths to keep new information from intruding. The larger the headquarters, the more it can resemble a great "Bat Cave," where people come in early in the morning, figuratively attach themselves to the ceiling, do the same thing, the same way, all day until they depart to renew themselves outside the company at dusk. Little of the real world intrudes during the day. And ideas tend to collect on the floor as "guano" for some consultant to mine.

If we are serious about business growth, the only way to counter these instincts is to embed information acquisition, processing and dissemination activities into the existing fabric of our operations. As previously discussed, at USAA, ECHO™ is integrated into the operational business system to ensure its availability to customer service people; therefore, it is an embedded feedback collection, analysis and dissemination activity. People can ignore the information it generates, but they can't hide it. Moreover, it is always visible to all levels of management, limiting the possibility of massive application of a "Group think" or spun outcome.

If we choose to activate an internal information clearing house to help us drive information, embedding the process is no more expensive; in fact, it is somewhat less expensive. We don't have to develop new systems and applications. Further, the payoff is the automatic integration of all inputs into the activities of the company. As the process evolves, so too can information activities. Long term, however, the value is a constant intrusion and infusion of new information into our daily deliberations so that our businesses can learn and renew themselves if the leadership wants them to.

5. *Failing to properly resource information gathering, processing, and dissemination activities.* Despite good intentions, unless appropriate resources are applied to the activity of information

Winning the Information Game

collection, processing, and dissemination, problems can and will arise. A company I visited had decided to create its information clearing house operations out of hide, using existing resources. In so doing, it made a new and unproven operation compete directly for resources with existing operations. The result was predictable—constant struggle, recurring personnel and systems problems, and lack of a departmental management structure that allowed effective day-to-day interface at the needed levels of company operations. Were it not for some early significant wins and absolute CEO and senior-level support, it is doubtful the department would have survived.

The departmental structure in any information collection, analysis, and dissemination effort needs to be established first. Moreover, it needs to conform with the existing company leadership structure. If the department head is going to interface with vice presidents and the department managers with executive directors, then they need to be of comparable grade and influence. Additionally, if departmental operations are going to use and leverage systems, then technical support needs to be available from the outset. Further, once the best estimate of people skills are determined, the best people need to be hired for information integration jobs without regard to other units or the temptation to skimp. Finally, training resources need to be identified and set aside for both departmental as well as company employee development. Failure to do so will result in continuing operational problems.

6. Failing to adapt to changing information needs. Information needs will always change. Conversely, much of the feedback that goes into making the information will not. At first glance this seems like a paradox. It isn't. But failure to understand the difference between the two can cause problems in meeting the needs of our information user customers within our company. Let me explain. There is a well-known business story about a car company whose analysts got so focused on its customer satisfaction ratings that the company almost went broke. Those that bought the cars always gave great ratings, but their dealers were selling fewer and fewer cars.

Avoid the Information Highway Potholes

The analysts had been collecting data on why people didn't buy the company's cars, and they knew that the demographics of their customers pointed to an increasingly narrow age-range appeal of their products, but they continued to provide only information from satisfied customers. Management had been asking the right questions but the information processing people hadn't heard, because they were too wrapped up in their existing activities. What they should have been doing was listening very closely to their internal customers and constantly repackaging the information for them.

The lesson for us here is that we need to make sure that the components of our information-processing operations do not become so fixed that they become outdated or irrelevant. Constant awareness of the activities of the business is an imperative. Recurring visits with managers who use the information also helps. And including the department in general business, staff, and operational deliberations offers insights about changing information needs.

Another way to avoid this pitfall is for us to always focus the processing capabilities of our clearing houses so that they are on the lookout for the new and different, and to make it available to customers. One thing to remember is that the job of an information processor is like that of a good fisherman. We must like to work areas where the water is smooth and calm. When a fish causes a ripple, we immediately cast to that point. When we discover and mine the value of the result, we then share it with others. In like manner, as information processors, we set up our processes, and then we constantly scan so that when the new or novel occurs, it is like the ripple in our fisherman's lake.

7. *Allowing information filters to spring up.* Just as a fisherman doesn't allow anything to get between him and his fish, so too must we as information collection, analysis, and dissemination users not allow information filters to spring up. When this happens the information loses clarity. Further, it is tougher to know the real value of the information. And it is almost impossible to be able to relate it to other information.

Winning the Information Game

Recall the childhood game of "telephone"? Here the first person in a line of people is told something and is asked to rapidly pass it on by whispering the information to the person next to him or her. When the message gets to the last person, he or she is asked to repeat it. Invariably, the message bears no resemblance to the original. In effect, the people in the line are a series of filters, each adding their own interpretation to the message. The same holds true in business information collection, integration and dissemination. The greater the number of filters, the greater the potential for business mistakes and failure. And no humor comes attached to these situations, as it does with the kid's game of "telephone."

Certainly, our information clearing houses can also be wrong in their collection, integration, and dissemination, but here the opportunity for exaggeration is limited; there is accountability, and we know where the corrective action must be taken. Moreover, if our information clearing houses have multiple sources of data and feedback coming in, the opportunity for internal verification and checking can reduce the chances for error.

On the output side, there are also advantages to limiting the number of filters between messengers and receivers. The faster and less attenuated is the information received, the better chance there is for an appropriate response. The effect is analogous to our automatic bodily responses, such as sweating when we're hot, mentioned earlier in this book. If the information about the need to sweat had been filtered, the person would have been more at risk.

8. Spinning or manipulating information. A very deadly information highway pothole grows out of the issue of information filters. It is our temptation to spin or manipulate information. The difference here is that messages are portrayed as if they are the transmitted, unfiltered information, when in reality, something has been left out or added to cause a different impression. Politicians might get away with such activities, but businesses who do it lose their ethical balance and trust with employees and customers. As a result, all company information activities can become suspect.

The power of information derives from its reliability, timeliness and applicability. If any one of these attributes is tampered with on purpose, everything is at risk. People depend on information because of its ability to clarify and promote effective action, no matter how painful. If an outcome has been decided in advance, and only information is being provided that promotes that outcome, then the messages being sent are no longer information; they are rather propaganda that seeks to manipulate. Our companies will ultimately lose the competitive battle.

9. Becoming the action agent rather than the information facilitator. The role of the information facilitator in the information age is very frustrating. From past vantage points in the business of taking feedback and turning it into information, I personally could see clearly some of the actions that might need to be taken to solve a problem. We must control the temptation to act. It's only a short step from relaying information to taking charge of the process. The only problem is that we rarely possess the capability, responsibility or expertise to sustain such activities. And frustration is a very poor excuse for forgetting that our task at all company levels is getting the information to the right place as fast as possible.

Time and time again we need to remind people that our information age task is providing good, timely information. There is no requirement to own the guilt that may come with the message or accept responsibility to do anything with the information provided. That responsibility belongs to the recipient.

We are all still caught up in industrial-age behaviors that are hard to break. In those days, problems were passed to experts who provided our management with templates and recommendations. They were the executive monkeys of business. They got the ulcers, and we got the bonuses. Further, with any luck they were kept locked in closed rooms, and we passed tasks on notes to them under the door. This might have been convenient, but this practice is irrelevant to the information age or the business of driving information.

10. Forgetting to reward good use of information. We do the things we get rewarded for. Let me repeat that—*We do the things we get rewarded for.* Too often our businesses talk about leveraging information for competitive advantage, but reward their employees for doing the exact opposite. When our companies fail the test of being able to fix things and promote solutions and results, we shouldn't be surprised.

Making sure that we reward people for using information is a continuous task, and one that requires a lot of hard work. Reward systems developed specifically to recognize and celebrate those who use information to fix things is one way to attack the problem. At a company I visited, employees can earn points when they fix something based on information provided which can be traded later for merchandise.

A business colleague told me about a company that had a unique way of rewarding employees for doing the right thing. The first time an employee gets complimented for doing a good job by customers, management or other employees, he or she gets a "winner's" bulletin board to hang in his or her work area. The next time, the worker is awarded a pin to go on the board. When a specified number of pins are received, a member of the company's senior management takes the employee out to lunch. Finally, an employee who takes significant action to improve things as a result of information provided joins a "Tiger's Club" and gets a bonus and a nice letter from the CEO. The point, of course, for everyone involved is to make sure words and actions match. If we say that doing something with information is important, then we need to recognize it in some way. If we don't, the behavior dies.

THE END OF THE ROAD

Winning and thriving as businesses in the information age is not something to fear, all admonitions aside. On the contrary, if we are willing to believe and be open with information, market domination is a certainty. Once again, we need to remember that the revolution is primarily internal. We must start by confronting it inside our own personal, professional worlds. The final answers are, therefore, to be found in our own concepts of business philosophy and practice.

The aim in this book has been to make this discussion useful, enlightening, and even humorous. Moreover, it is my earnest hope that all your businesses will take the seven steps needed to win and adapt to the information age. Sadly, I must report that I am skeptical. In spite of those who wish otherwise, the seeds of business failure will always be internal, personal, and within the minds of the people themselves who make up our companies. Regardless of the talent of our employees, or the promise of some computer whiz, business practice in the main has always been an art and will remain so. We only need to look at the problem in the stress-induced images of IBM, Kodak, Apple Computers and Eastern Airlines (remember them?), to mention only a few.

If we read and heed what has been written, such outcomes need not be inevitable. In this regard, my dad, an insightful New Englander, gave me some advice years ago that I pass on as my parting words. On the side of a hill toward the center of a small town in northern Vermont where I spent my youth, on the right side of the road, sits a spring-fed watering trough. As my father and I passed by that watering trough on a summer's day many years ago, my father told me: "Son, that water trough will always be a part of this town because it reminds us all of one basic truth. Our job in life is to grow, learn, and share, always remembering our job is to get the horse to water. It's the horse's job to drink."

APPENDIX A

PROACTIVE VERSUS REACTIVE THINKING

PROACTIVE	*REACTIVE*
Problem-centered	Person-centered
Positive	Negative
Offensive	Defensive
Us	We-They
Partnering	Adversarial
Inclusive	Exclusive
Hand clasping	Finger pointing
Sharing	Secretive
Exploratory	Fault finding
Win/Win	Win/Lose
Anticipatory	After-the-fact
Creative	Dogmatic
Flexible	Rigid

APPENDIX B

CHARACTERISTICS OF INFORMATION-DRIVING AND LEVERGING BUSINESSES

- Work is problem-focused. Employees work informally and are not preoccupied with status, turf, or second-guessing their bosses.
- Innovative behavior is encouraged and rewarded.
- Employees freely signal their awareness of difficulties because they know the problems will be handled and solved.
- A sense of the positive and a focus on outcomes dominate work attitudes at all levels.
- Goals are shared by all levels of the business, and there is a strong and consistent flow of activity toward achieving excellence.
- Decision making is anticipatory and is determined by such factors as information availability, employee skills, a shared sense of responsibility, timing, and requirements for team and individual development.
- A natural balance exists between team and individual effort in planning, performance, and outcomes.
- Collaboration is prevalent. Employees readily request help and are willing to help in return.
- Differing opinions are respected and considered important to business responsiveness to information inputs.
- There is a great deal of on-the-job information-driven learning, based on a willingness to give, seek, and use feedback.
- Relationships are honest and not political. Employees care about one another and do not feel isolated.
- Employees are involved and motivated by choice. Their attitudes reflect an open exploratory stance. They are optimistic, seeing work as important and fun.
- A high degree of trust exists among all levels of the company, accompanied by a sense of freedom and mutual responsibility.

Winning the Information Game

- Poor performance is confronted and joint solutions developed.
- Caring and support are directed with a firm focus on the work needing attention.
- A sense of order is leveraged in ways that promote high levels of innovation and creativity.
- The business adapts swiftly to opportunities or threats because information is valued and used to fix things and facilitate solutions and results.
- Business structure, procedures and policies are seen as tools to help employees get the job done and to help focus effort. They can and do change as the situation demands.
- Leadership and management are flexible, shifting in style and emphasis to meet the situation.
- Technology and equipment are seen as tools to be leveraged and used in support of business objectives, and not as ends in themselves.
- Change is accepted as part of a never-ending quest for business stability and balance.
- There is a natural harmony between human and physical business systems.

REFERENCES AND SUGGESTED READINGS

Adams, Scott. *Dogbert's Management Handbook*. New York: Harper Business, 1996.

Barlow, Janelle and Claus Moeller. *A Complaint is a Gift*. San Francisco: Berrett- Koehler Publications,1996.

Bennis, Warren, and Burt Nanus. *Leaders: The Strategies for Taking Charge*. New York: Harper and Row, 1985.

Blattberg, Robert C., Rashi Glazer and John D.C. Little. *The Marketing Information Revolution*. Boston, MA: Harvard Business School Press, 1994.

Cairncross, Frances. *The Death of Distance*. Boston MA: Harvard Business School Press, 1997.

Davenport, Thomas H. and Laurence Prusak. *Working Knowledge*. Boston, MA: Harvard Business School Press, 1998.

Dow, Roger and Susan Cook. *Turned On*. New York: Harper Business, 1996.

Downes, Larry and Chunka Mui. *Unleashing the Killer App digital strategies for market dominance*. Boston, MA: Harvard Business School Press, 1998.

Hammer, Michael. *Beyond Reengineering.* New York: Harper Business, 1996.

Hiebeler, Robert, Thomas B. Kelly, and Charles Ketteman. *Best Practices: Building Your Business with Customer-Focused Solutions*. New York: Simon & Schuster, 1998.

Hildebrand, Carol. "Satisfaction Guaranteed." *CIO Magazine*, August 1995, www.cio.com.

Kelly, Kevin. *Out of Control*. Reading, MA: Addison-Wesley, 1994.

McKenna, Regis. *Real Time*. Boston, MA: Harvard Business School Press, 1997.

Musashi, Miyamoto. *A Book of Five Rings*. Woodstock, N.Y.: The overlook Press, 1982.

Patton, George S., Jr. *War As I Knew It*. Annotated by Paul D. Harkins, Boston: Houghton Mifflin Co., 1947.

Peters, Tom. *Thriving on Chaos*. New York: Alfred A. Knopf, 1987.

Petzinger, Thomas, Jr. "The Front Lines." *The Wall Street Journal*, September 27, 1996, p. B1.

Petzinger, Thomas, Jr. "Forget Empowerment, This Job Requires Constant Brainpower." *The Wall Street Journal*, October 17, 1997, p. B1.

Ringenbach, Paul T. *USAA A Tradition of Service 1922-1997*. Dallas: The Donning Co., 1997.

Shelton, Ken. *Beyond Counterfeit Leadership*. Provo, UT: Executive Excellence Press, 1998.

The Futures Group. "Ostriches & Eagles." A report by the Futures Group, Glastonbury, CT July, 1995.

Timmerman, Frederick W., Jr. "ECHO System Helps USAA Listen —and Respond—to Customer Feedback." *Journal of Retail Banking Services*, Summer 1998, p. 29.

Timmerman, Frederick W., Jr. "Industry Can Profit From Feedback Engineering." *Best'sReview* (P&C Edition), July 1996, p. 96.

Timmerman, Frederick W., Jr. "Yes, Sir! General Machine, Sir!" *Army Magazine,* January, 1982, p. 30.

Unruh, James A. *Customers Mean Business.* Reading, MA: Addison-Wesley, 1996.

U.S. Army Field Manual 22-103, *Leadership andCommand at Senior Levels,* Washington, D.C.: U.S. Government Printing Office, 1987. (Frederick W. Timmerman, Jr.)

U.S. Federal Benchmarking Consortium Study Report. *Serving the American Public: Best Practices in One-Stop Customer Service,* Washington, D.C.: U.S. Government Printing Office, November, 1997.

Weber, Thomas E. "Simplest E-Mail Queries Confound Companies." *The Wall Street Journal,* October 21, 1996, p. B1.

Webster, Frederick E. *Market Driven Management.* New York: John Wiley & Sons, Inc., 1994.

Wilhelm, Wayne and Bill Rossello. "The Care and Feeding of Customers." *Management Review,* March, 1997, p. 19.

Wing, Michael J. *Talking with your Customers.* Dearborn, MI: Enterprise, 1993.

Zaleznik, Abraham. "Real Work." *Harvard Business Review,* November-December, (1997), p. 53.

Winning the Information Game

Dr. Frederick W. (Tim) Timmerman, Jr. is COO of Direct1. He is a graduate of the United States Military Academy, has served in many sensitive, high-level government and international positions, and holds an MA and PhD from Duke University. He is the author of over 30 professional articles and technical papers dealing with military leadership, information integration, and organizational development issues.

Prior to joining Direct1, Tim spent nine years in executive management at USAA. Most recently, he was head of USAA's Department of Member Relations and Feedback. In recognition of its efforts, his department received Arthur Anderson's 1997 Worldwide Best Practices Award for customer satisfaction excellence. Tim lives in North Carolina with his wife, Susan. They have four children, Eric, Erin, Tracey, and Cindy.

ABOUT DIRECT1

Direct1 deploys and sustains world-class, real-time/continuous and adaptable feedback systems, equipping businesses to dominate their markets through immediate application of precise, actionable, operational information that responds to customer, competitor, and employee needs and actions.

For this reason, Direct1 has emerged as the leader in the customized expert systems design, development, and deployment of continuous feedback, analysis, and advisory technologies. Many of the world's largest conglomerates are working with Direct1 in developing early warning, customer-feedback, and employee-management solutions for their markets.

To contact Direct1, visit its Web site at www.direct1.com, or call (704) 849-6942.

INDEX

Alabama, 22
Allowing Information to get personal, 145
Analysis, 137
Apple Computers, 153
Arthur Andersen Consulting
    Andersen Associates Hiebeler, Kelly, and Kettelman, 89
    WorldWide Customer Satisfaction Best Practices Award, 89
AT&T, 43
AT&T Universal Card (Universal Card Services), 88
Battles, Brett, 34
Becoming the message instead of the messenger, 144
Best Practices: Building Your Business with Customer-Focused Solutions (Hiebeler, Kelly, and Kettelman), 89
Bests' Review, 90, 91
Beyond Counterfeit Leadership (Shelton), 36
Beyond Reengineering (Hammer), 35
Biology
    And feedback, 37, 78, 106, 113
    And Information Processing, 64, 83, 117
Book Structure, 20-21
Burning Platforms, 34
Business @ the Speed of Thought (Gates), 38
Business Learning, 81
Business Schools and Skills Training, 130
Business Systems
    Cohesion in, 49
    Diagnosis of, 99, 100
    Failures of, 53-56, 112-113, 116, 146, 148-149
    Hierarchical/stovepipe, 31, 62
    Information-leveraged, 31
Business Vision as:
    Management tool, 44-45
    Means to focus effort, 45
    Organizing principal, 44
    Reference point, 44
Cairncross, Frances, 32, 59

Caller ID, 35
Cell Phones, 43
Center for Army Lessons Learned (CALL), 81
CEO's and Coordination, 135
CEO's and Shared Vision, 42
Change Business, 23, 29
    Historical, 31
    Personal, 18-20
    Technological, 29
Characteristics of Information-driving and Leveraging Businesses, 155-156
Charts
    Interactivity Means, 58
    Integration Choices, 61
    Feedback is a Highly Valued but Perishable Resource, 75
    Steps in Starting an Information Clearing House, 83
    The ECHO™ System at Work, 97
    Direct1's Total Feedback System Process, 101
    Information Feedback Loop, 121
Churchill, Winston, 111
Coca-Cola, 60
Communications Segmentation, 57
"Companies that Just Don't Get It," Wall Street Journal, 34
"Companies can Benefit from Feedback Engineering," Bests' Review, 90
Competitive Intelligence, 64, 89
Computer Sciences Corporation (CSC)
    CSC and CRM, 102
    Description, 90
    Direct1 and CSC, 102-103
    Help Desk Test, 102-104
Count, Analyze, Fix versus Fix, Count, Analyze, 38, 108, 114-115
CSC Help Desk, 101-104
Customer
    Needs, 62
    Preferences, 54, 57-58
    Use of Technology, 34-35

Winning the Information Game

Customer Relationship Management (CRM), 101
Cyberworld, 126
Data Bases
    Differences from Data Warehouses, 71
    Proliferation of, 70
Declaration of Independence, 42
Definitions
    Active versus Passive Feedback Collection, 78
    Data Warehouse, 24
    Facilitators, 119
    Feedback System, 23
    Information, 64, 67
    Information Clearing House, 24
    Information Integration, 60-61
    Information Interactivity, 57
    Information Inventory, 64
    Manipulation, 135
    Persuasion, 135
    Real Teams, 119
    Relationship Skills, 129
    Shared Vision, 42-43
    Systems Teams, 120
    Virtual Teams, 119
Deming, W. Edwards, 17
Diagnostic Business tools, 99
Digital electronic pathways, 32, 127
Digital Equipment Corporation, 22
Direct1, the external example
    Aims and purpose, 90, 99
    AutoQuest™, 99
    Capabilities, 99
    External Clearing House described, 98-101
    Operational characteristics, 98-99, 118
    Smart Alerts, 106
Downes, Larry, 73
Eastern Airlines, 153
ECHO™
    ECHO™ at USAA, 94-98
    "ECHO System Helps USAA Listen-and Respond-to Customer Feedback," (*Journal of Retail Banking Services*), 93
    Operation of, 95-96
    Systems, 96, 147
    HOT TOPICS, 97-98
Einstein, Albert, 53
Emerson, Ralph Waldo, 41
Essential Elements of Information(EEI), 115, 119, 124
Establishing Business Purpose, 46
Executive Skill Development Gaps, 127
Explicit versus Implicit management, 35-37
Failing to Embed Information Activities, 146

Failure to resource feedback/information gathering, 147-148
Feedback
    Active versus Passive, 78
    Adaptability, 100
    Collection, 64, 67, 77-79
    Confidentiality, 145
    Customers, 75-76, 88
    Digital, 18
    Early Warning, 95, 100
    Emphasis, 77
    Employee, 73-74, 81, 88, 95
    Fear of, 38, 104,105
    Management of, 34, 92-93, 94, 144
    Personal, 20
    Organic, 26, 37, 78
    Real time, 99, 102-103
    Senior support, 91, 148
    Visibility, 96
    Volumes, 94
Feedback Loops, 84, 94, 96-97, 121-122
Finger Pointing and blame placing, 145
Ford Motor Company, 88
Fortune magazine, 87, 135
Fuld & Co., 64
Futures Group, "Ostriches and Eagles," 89
Gates, Bill, 38, 70
General Electric, 88
Gulf of Mexico, 22
Hammer, Michael, 35
Harvard Business Press, 39
Harvard Business Review, 127
Herres, General Robert, 91
Hitler's Blitzkrieg, 31
IBM, 153
Information Bat Caves, 147
Information Clearing Houses
    As a feedback loop, 80-81
    As facilitators, 72, 143
    As processors, 62-63, 149
    Fostering Communications, 76
    Functions, 77-82
    Integration, 92, 105
    Lessons Learned, 104-107
    Promoting Solutions and Results, 92
    Operations of, 84-85
    Organic/Biological, 37, 78,
    Organization, 78
    Responsibilities, 71-76
    Shooting the Messenger, 72, 93, 144
    Starting a Clearing House, 82-83
    Training, 93, 105, 108, 124
    Value of, 69, 117,
    Use of Data Warehouses, 79
Information/Data
    Business payoff, 24-26, 122-123

Index

Control of, 26, 33, 35
Facilitators/Facilitation, 26, 72, 119-120, 151
Filters, 149
Gridlock, 70
Hiding, 46, 116, 117
Integration, 55
Interactivity, 57-59
Inventory, 64
Manipulation, 47, 127, 150
Neutrality, 144
Overload, 19-20, 33-34, 70
Politics of, 104, 131
Sharing, 50, 81, 116, 117-118
Skills gaps, 93, 106-107, 126
Time-driven value of, 74-75
Types of, 26
Waste, 64, 98
Information Principles
  Act Simultaneously, 113-114
  Be redundant, 113
  Change the Action Order, 114
  Develop a Business Focus, 115
  Keep Information Visible, 116
  Link Feedback Loops, 121-122
  Package for Use, 118-119
  Reward, 120-121, 151-152
  Share, 117-118
  Summary of, 124
  Use Facilitators, 119-120
  Watch and Listen, 112-113
Information Survival Skills
  Analytical Skills, 136-139, 140
    Assessment, 136-137
    Decision-making, 137-138
    Forecasting, 138
    Intuition, 138-139
  Facilitation Skills, 133-136, 140
    Coordination, 134-135, 143
    Endurance, 134
    Persuasion, 135-136
    Risk-Taking, 134
  Relationship Skills, 128-133, 140
    Interpersonal, 132-133
    Listening, 132
    Perspective, 130-131
    Teaching/Coaching, 131-132
Internal Information barriers
  Attitudinal, 38-39, 104, 108
  Operational, 35-38
  Technological, 31-34
Internet and Feedback, 103
Internet Humor
  Bosses, 118,
  Businessmen and Ballooning, 71
  Clients, 132-133

Consultants, 18
  New Employees, 111, 131
  Engineers, 19
  Landscape Workers, 125
  MBA Graduates, 133
  Psychics, 77
  Quotes, 45
  The Business Professional, 30, 128
  The Parrot and the Business Person, 126
Intranet and employees, 33
Journal of Retail Banking Services, 93
Knowledge Management, 39, 81
Kodak, 153
Leadership
  "And" versus "Either/Or," 50, 107
  Direction, 47-48
  Ethical, 44, 49
  Goals and Standards, 48
  Moral, 44
  Motivation, 48-49
  Purpose, 46-47
  Teams, 50
  Values, 48, 131
  Will, 44
Leadership and Command at Senior Levels (US Army), 42
Maginot Line, 31
Manager concerns, 17, 131
Mark, David, 34
Master Chess Players and Information, 138
Medical diagnosis and Feedback, 99, 100
Mencken, H.L., 141
Mercedes-Benz, 60
MCI, 60
Microsoft Power Point, 129
Military Leadership and Shared Vision, 42
Monarch Marking Systems, 47
Mui, Chunka, 73
Nicklaus, Jack, 69
Not adapting to changing information needs, 148
Olson, Ken, 22
One way Communications, 142-143
Patton, General George, 23
Payoff for Winning the Game, 24-27
PeaPod, 57
Personal insecurity, 33
Petzinger, Thomas, 88
Pillsbury, 88
Plantation Leadership, 36
Pony Express, 31
Positive Business Climate, 77, 104
Pre-boomers, 54
Prentice Hall, 39
Proactive versus Reactive Thinking, 154

Winning the Information Game

Promontory Point, Utah, 31
Proactive versus Reactive thinking, 37
"Real Work," (*Harvard Business Review*),
    127, 130
Ringenbach, Paul, 91
Roosevelt, Eleanor, 87
Sears and Roebuck, 32
Senses and Feedback, 115
Shakespeare and attitudes, 144
Shared Vision
    Activities, 45-49
    Characteristics, 44-45
    Implementation, 49-51
Shelton, Ken, 36, 38
Soccer and Information Skills, 131
Southwest Airlines, 87-88
Stovepipe processes, 60
Synthesis, 137
TARP, 112
Technology and
    Biology, 37
    Business, 32
Telegraph, 31
The Death of Distance (Cairncross), 32, 59
Third Voice Software, 35
Trust, 39, 49, 78
Truth with a capital "T", 138
Twain, Mark, 29
Underestimating the Impact of Attitudes,
    142-144
United States Army, 42, 81
*Unleashing the Killer App, Digital Strategies
for Market Dominance* (Downes&Mui),
    73
USAA, 59, 89, 99, 99, 104
USAA and Feedback, 90
USAA, the inside clearing house example,
    90-98
USAA, A Tradition of Service, 1922-1977
    (Ringenbach), 91
US Senate and computers, 18
Vision-driven Marketing, 43
Wall Street Journal, 34, 47, 60, 64, 98
Word of Mouth, 35
Working Knowledge (Davenport&Prusak), 39
Wright, Wilbur, 125
Zaleznik, Abraham, 127, 128, 130
3M Company, 60